THE POWER OF POSITIVE THINKING

Train Your Brain To Create A Life You Love

RACHEL STONE

Copyright © 2023 by Rachel Stone

All rights reserved.

No part of this book may be reproduced in any form or by any electronic or mechanical means, including information storage and retrieval systems, without written permission from the author, except for the use of brief quotations in a book review.

Other books By Rachel Stone

Develop the power of positive thinking TODAY!

Other books by Rachel Stone

RACHEL STONE
WHAT CONFIDENT *Women Do*

9 STEPS TO ULTIMATE SELF-CONFIDENCE

Discover the 9 steps to ultimate self-confidence TODAY!

Other books by Rachel Stone

Stop people-pleasing and doubting. A friendly guide to dealing with toxic relationships and gaslighting. Start living, healing and being the best version of yourself TODAY!

Other books by Rachel Stone

Get the tools to break free from self-absorbed and emotionally abusive family members. Let go of the need for approval and learn to love yourself. Embark on a journey of acceptance and be happy again TODAY!

Other books by Rachel Stone

Get anxiety relief from people-pleasing. Stop dimming your light for others. Dare to set boundaries and live your best life with courage, freedom and without apologies TODAY!

Other books by Rachel Stone

RACHEL STONE
WHY LIVING A SIMPLE LIFE IS BETTER *For You*

THROUGH DECLUTTERING, MINIMALISM AND STREAMLINING, FINALLY START ENJOYING A MEANINGFUL LIFE

Through decluttering, minimalism and streamlining, finally start enjoying a meaningful life TODAY!

Other books by Rachel Stone

Get your friendly guide to living a fabulous life feeling free and happy TODAY!

Other books by Rachel Stone

Stop your negative thinking in its tracks. New practical strategies to master your mind and block your intrusive thoughts, even if you've tried it all before. Take back control TODAY!

Contents

Introduction	xxiii
How You Will Benefit From This Book	xxv

1. WHAT IS POSITIVE THINKING? — 1
- Famous 'positive thinkers' — 2
- Why do we like to be around positive people? — 2

2. But Why Is Positive Thinking So Difficult? — 4
3. Most Popular Questions On 'Positive Thinking' — 6
4. Myths Around Positive Thinking — 10
5. RESILIENCE: ACCEPTING AND OVERCOMING ADVERSITY — 14
- What is adversity? — 14
- What is resilience? — 14
- 10 things you can do today to practice resilience — 16

6. POSITIVE THINKING AND MENTAL HEALTH — 18
- Understanding the impact of negative thinking on mental health — 18
- Strategies for coping with negative thoughts — 19
- Behaviours to watch out for — 20
- Easy ways to start improving today — 20

7. COGNITIVE BEHAVIOURAL THERAPY AND POSITIVE THINKING — 22
- The history of CBT — 23
- The Cognitive Model — 23
- Techniques for promoting positive thinking — 24
- Practical applications of CBT and positive thinking — 24
- The CBT principles — 24
- What you can start doing today — 26
- Where can you get CBT treatment? — 27

8. POSITIVE THINKING AND SUCCESS — 29
- Defining success — 30
- Myths about positive thinking and success — 31

Strategies for incorporating positive thinking into goal-setting and action-taking ... 31
Tips for overcoming obstacles and staying positive ... 32

9. **THE IMPORTANCE OF MINDFULNESS AND MEDITATION ON POSITIVE THINKING** ... 34
   The history of mindfulness and meditation ... 35
   The benefits of mindfulness and meditation ... 36
   Practical tips and strategies for incorporating mindfulness and meditation into daily life ... 36
   Questions and answers ... 37

10. **PRACTISING GRATITUDE AND APPRECIATION** ... 41
    Understanding the benefits of gratitude and appreciation ... 41
    Actionable steps for practising gratitude and appreciation ... 42
    Starting today ... 43

11. **POSITIVE THINKING AND BUILDING RELATIONSHIPS** ... 45
    Defining positive thinking in relationships ... 46
    Myths about positive thinking and building relationships ... 47
    Strategies for incorporating positive thinking into building and maintaining relationships ... 48
    Tips for overcoming obstacles and staying positive in relationships ... 49
    Common questions and challenges in building positive relationships ... 50

12. Practical Ways To Make Your Relationship More Positive: ... 52

13. **THE DANGERS OF NEGATIVE THINKING** ... 55
    Defining negative thinking ... 55
    Understanding the root cause of negative thinking ... 56
    Causes of negative thinking ... 57
    Physical effects of negative thinking ... 57
    Psychological effects of negative thinking ... 58

14. UNDERSTANDING NEGATIVE PEOPLE - AND HOW TO AVOID THEM ... 60
    Defining negative people ... 60
    Common questions and challenges ... 61

15. BREAKING FREE: STRATEGIES FOR OVERCOMING NEGATIVE THOUGHTS ... 64
    Strategies for overcoming negative thoughts ... 64
    Tips for maintaining a positive mindset ... 65

16. STEPPING OUT OF YOUR COMFORT ZONE ... 67
    The benefits of coming out of your comfort zone ... 68
    How people feel before and after coming out of their comfort zone ... 68
    How you can start today ... 69
    25 small ways anybody can come out of their comfort zone today ... 70
    How will this help me feel more positive? ... 71

17. LIMITING BELIEFS ... 73
    Do you have limiting beliefs? ... 73
    Where do limiting beliefs come from? ... 75
    The impact of limiting beliefs ... 76
    Strategies for overcoming limiting beliefs ... 76
    The value of overcoming limiting beliefs ... 78

18. WHAT IF OUR PARENTS INFLUENCED OUR LIMITING BELIEFS? ... 79
    Understanding the root causes ... 79
    Signs and symptoms of parent-influenced limiting beliefs ... 80
    The consequences of not challenging parent-influenced limiting beliefs ... 80
    Strategies for overcoming parent-influenced limiting beliefs ... 80
    Repairing the relationship ... 81

19. Pursue Your Passions - Be A Kid Again! ... 83
20. Why Do We Feel We Can't "Be A Kid?" ... 85
21. Hobby Ideas To Live A More Positive Life ... 87
22. CREATE A BUCKET LIST – FEEL AMAZING! ... 92
    Some myths about creating a bucket list ... 93
    Some bucket list ideas ... 94

23. WRITING A PRIORITY LIST		96
Why is a priority list more effective than a long to-do list?		96
Your weekly/monthly priority list		97
24. Conclusion		104
Other books By Rachel Stone		107
Other books by Rachel Stone		109
Other books by Rachel Stone		111
Other books by Rachel Stone		113
Other books by Rachel Stone		115
Other books by Rachel Stone		117
Other books by Rachel Stone		119
Other books by Rachel Stone		121

Introduction

Welcome to **The Power Of Positive Thinking**. This book is for anyone who has ever struggled with negative thoughts and the impact they can have on our lives.

In this book, we will explore the true meaning of positive thinking and why it can be so difficult to achieve. We will discuss the importance of resilience, and how to accept and overcome adversity. We will also delve into the connection between positive thinking and mental health, as well as the link between positive thinking and success.

We will also cover the benefits of cognitive behavioural therapy and positive thinking, and the role of mindfulness and meditation in promoting positive thinking. Additionally, we will explore the importance of practising gratitude and appreciation, and the impact of positive thinking on building relationships.

We will also examine the dangers of negative thinking and the physical and psychological effects it can have on our lives. We will also explore the cognitive processes and their effects.

We will provide strategies for overcoming negative thoughts, understanding negative people and how to avoid them, and overcoming limiting beliefs. We will also look at how our parents may have influenced our limiting beliefs.

Within this book, we will discuss the benefits of coming out of your comfort zone and ways to achieve this. We will also provide tips on training your brain to think more positively, get into positive habits, and design the life you deserve. We will also explore the positive effects of pursuing your passions and provide hobby ideas for leading a more positive life. Finally, we will discuss the value of goal setting for a more positive life.

Join us as we challenge the myths and misconceptions surrounding positive thinking and empower ourselves to live our best lives.

How You Will Benefit From This Book

After reading this book on positive thinking, you will be equipped with the tools and strategies you need to shift your focus to the good in every situation. You will learn how to overcome negative thoughts and limiting beliefs that may have been holding you back. You will also learn how to be more resilient in the face of adversity, and to see challenges as opportunities to grow and learn.

By practising the techniques outlined in this book, you will be able to improve your mental health, increase your success and feel more fulfilled in your life. You will learn the benefits of mindfulness, meditation and gratitude and how to use them to promote positive thinking.

You will also learn how to identify and avoid negative people and situations, and how to come out of your comfort zone to pursue your passions and design the life you deserve. You will learn the value of goal setting for a more positive life.

Overall, you will come away from this book with a renewed sense of hope and optimism, and the ability to see the good in every situation. You will be more resilient and better equipped to handle challenges that come your way. You will be more successful, happier and more fulfilled in your life.

What Is Positive Thinking?

Positive thinking is the practice of focusing on the good in a situation and maintaining a hopeful attitude. It means looking for the silver lining in difficult situations, and believing that things will turn out well in the end.

For example, instead of thinking *"I'll never be able to do this"* when faced with a challenging task, a positive thinker would say *"I can do this, I just need to keep trying."*

Another example would be in a difficult relationship, instead of thinking *"I can't stand this person, they always bring me down"* a positive thinker would think *"I may not agree with everything this person does, but I choose to focus on the good in this relationship and what they bring to my life."*

Positive thinking is not just about being happy all the time or ignoring negative emotions, but it's about shifting our focus to the good in every situation and looking for opportunities to grow and learn.

Famous 'positive thinkers'

Many famous people have been known for their positive thinking and optimism. Some examples include:

Oprah Winfrey: Oprah is known for her ability to overcome adversity and has spoken publicly about the importance of positive thinking in her life.

Tony Robbins: Tony Robbins is a motivational speaker and self-help author who is known for his positive thinking and can-do attitude.

Louise Hay: Louise Hay is a self-help author and motivational speaker who is known for her positive affirmations and the power of positive thinking.

Abraham Lincoln: Abraham Lincoln is famous for his positive attitude during difficult times, and his famous quote *"I am not concerned that you have fallen—I am concerned that you arise."*

Norman Vincent Peale: Norman Vincent Peale is a pastor and self-help author who is known for his book "The Power of Positive Thinking" which has helped many people to change their mindset and improve their lives.

Confucius: Confucius was a Chinese philosopher who emphasised the importance of positive thinking and the power of optimism in his teachings.

Why do we like to be around positive people?

There are several reasons why people tend to like being around those who are positive:

Positive energy: Positive people exude a sense of energy and optimism that can be contagious. Being around them can make us feel more energised and motivated.

Emotional support: Positive people are often more supportive and understanding, which can make us feel more comfortable opening up to them and sharing our thoughts and feelings.

Positivity is contagious: Positive thinking is contagious, meaning that when we spend time with positive people, their positive attitude tends to rub off on us and we start to think and see things more positively.

Problem-solving: Positive people tend to be more proactive and solution-focused, rather than dwelling on problems. They can help us to see challenges as opportunities and to look for ways to overcome them.

2

But Why Is Positive Thinking So Difficult?

Positive thinking can be difficult for some people because it goes against our natural tendency to focus on negative thoughts and emotions. Our brains are wired to pay attention to negative information as a survival mechanism, this is known as the negativity bias. This means that it's easier for us to remember negative experiences and to dwell on negative thoughts.

Additionally, some people may have experienced traumatic events or grew up in a negative environment which can make it hard to change their negative thought patterns.

Also, negative thoughts can become a habit, and habits are hard to break. When we think negatively, we may be more likely to experience negative emotions like stress, anxiety, and depression, which can make it even harder to think positively.

Moreover, societal and cultural factors can play a role in making positive thinking difficult. In some cultures, it's not seen as acceptable to express positive emotions or to be optimistic about the future.

Lastly, some people may not have the necessary tools or knowledge to practise positive thinking effectively. They may not know how to recognise negative thoughts, or how to replace them with positive ones.

In short, positive thinking can be difficult because of our natural tendency to focus on negative thoughts, past experiences, negative thought patterns, societal and cultural factors and lack of knowledge on how to practice it effectively. It requires effort, practice, and patience to overcome these obstacles and develop a more positive mindset.

3

Most Popular Questions On 'Positive Thinking'

Q. How can I develop a more positive mindset?

A. Developing a more positive mindset requires effort, practice, and patience. Some ways to develop a more positive mindset include: practising gratitude and appreciation, surrounding yourself with positive people, setting and achieving goals, and learning to recognise and replace negative thoughts with positive ones.

Q. What are the benefits of positive thinking?

A. The benefits of positive thinking include improved mental and physical health, increased resilience and ability to cope with stress and adversity, better relationships, improved performance and success, and greater overall well-being.

Q. How can positive thinking improve my mental health?

A. Positive thinking can improve mental health by reducing stress and anxiety, and by increasing feelings of happiness and well-being. When we think positively, we are more likely to experience positive emotions like joy and contentment, and less likely to experience negative emotions like stress and anxiety.

Q. How can positive thinking improve my physical health?

A. Positive thinking can improve physical health by reducing stress and inflammation, which can lead to a host of health problems. Positive thinking can also improve the immune system and increase the production of endorphins which can reduce pain and improve overall well-being.

Q. How can I practise gratitude and appreciation?

A. Practising gratitude and appreciation can be as simple as taking a few minutes each day to reflect on the things in your life that you are grateful for. You can also write a gratitude journal, or try to find something to appreciate in every situation. Additionally, expressing gratitude and appreciation to others can strengthen relationships and bring more positivity to your life.

Q. How can I surround myself with positive people?

A. Surrounding yourself with positive people can be as simple as seeking out and spending time with people who have a positive outlook on life. It can also mean limiting time with people who are negative and actively seeking out people who inspire and motivate you.

Q. How can setting and achieving goals improve my positive thinking?

A. Setting and achieving goals can improve positive thinking by providing a sense of purpose and direction. When we have something to work towards, it can give us a sense of motivation and accomplishment. Achieving our goals can also boost our self-esteem and confidence.

Q. How can I recognise and replace negative thoughts?

A. Recognising negative thoughts can be as simple as paying attention to how you feel and what you're thinking. Once you've identified a negative thought, try to replace it with a more positive thought. For example, if you find yourself thinking *"I'm not good enough,"* try to replace that thought with *"I am capable and will do my best."*

Q. How does positive thinking impact my relationships?

A. Positive thinking can improve relationships by making us more open, understanding, and supportive of others. When we think positively, we are more likely to see the good in others and build stronger connections.

Q. How can I use mindfulness and meditation to promote positive thinking?

A. Mindfulness and meditation can be effective tools for promoting positive thinking by helping us to focus on the present moment and to quiet the mind. This can help to reduce stress, anxiety, and negative thoughts and emotions.

Q. What is the connection between positive thinking and success?

A. Positive thinking can lead to greater success by helping us to overcome obstacles, to set and achieve goals, and build stronger relationships. Positive thinking can also improve our performance by increasing our confidence and motivation.

Q. How can I use cognitive behavioural therapy (CBT) to improve my positive thinking?

A. Cognitive behavioural therapy (CBT) is a form of psychotherapy that can be used to improve positive thinking by helping us to identify and change negative thought patterns. CBT can help us to recognise and replace negative thoughts with more positive and realistic ones.

Q. Why is it important to practise gratitude and appreciation?

A. Practising gratitude and appreciation can improve our overall well-being by helping us to focus on the good in our lives and to appreciate the things we have, rather than dwelling on what we lack. Gratitude can also improve our relationships and increase our feelings of happiness and contentment.

4

Myths Around Positive Thinking

Myth: Positive thinking means ignoring negative thoughts and emotions.

Truth: Positive thinking doesn't mean ignoring negative thoughts and emotions, but it means acknowledging them and healthily processing them. It's important to acknowledge and process negative thoughts and feelings so that we can learn from them and move on.

Myth: Positive thinking means always being happy.

Truth: Positive thinking doesn't mean always being happy, it's about having a balanced and realistic outlook on life. It's natural to experience a wide range of emotions, including sadness, anger, and disappointment. Positive thinking helps to put those emotions in perspective and to find the positive in any situation.

Myth: Positive thinking is only for optimistic people.

Truth: Positive thinking is for everyone, regardless of their personality or disposition. It's a skill that can be learned and practised by anyone who wants to improve their outlook on life.

Myth: Positive thinking is not necessary because things will work out on their own.

Truth: Positive thinking is a powerful tool that can help us to achieve our goals and to create the life we want. It can help us to see challenges as opportunities, and to take action to create positive change in our lives.

Myth: Positive thinking is only for people who want to be successful.

Truth: Positive thinking is not just for people who want to be successful, it's for anyone who wants to improve their overall well-being and quality of life.

Myth: Positive thinking is only for people who don't have serious problems.

Truth: Positive thinking can be especially helpful for people who are dealing with difficult challenges or problems. It can help to increase resilience and to see challenges as opportunities to grow and learn.

Myth: Positive thinking means pretending that everything is okay.

Truth: Positive thinking doesn't mean pretending that everything is okay when it's not. It means acknowledging and facing reality, but also choosing to focus on the good and find solutions, rather than dwelling on the negative.

Myth: Positive thinking is about being unrealistic and putting on a facade.

Truth: Positive thinking is about having a realistic and balanced outlook on life. It's not about ignoring problems or pretending they don't exist, but about finding ways to overcome them.

Myth: Positive thinking is only for certain situations and not for others.

Truth: Positive thinking can be applied to any situation, whether it's personal or professional, large or small. It's a mindset that can be applied to any area of life.

Myth: Positive thinking means you'll never have negative thoughts again.

Truth: Positive thinking doesn't mean you'll never have negative thoughts again, it's a practice and it takes time to change the negative thought patterns.

Myth: Positive thinking is about being perfect and never making mistakes.

Truth: Positive thinking is about learning from mistakes and accepting imperfections. It's about being kind and compassionate to oneself.

Myth: Positive thinking is about ignoring problems and hoping they'll go away.

Truth: Positive thinking is about facing problems head-on and finding solutions. It's about having a proactive and problem-solving attitude.

Myth: Positive thinking is only for naturally optimistic people.

Truth: Positive thinking is a skill that can be learned and practised by anyone, regardless of their natural disposition.

Myth: Positive thinking is only for a certain age group or stage in life.

Truth: Positive thinking can be beneficial at any age and stage in life. It's a mindset and a skill that can be learned and practised by people of all ages and backgrounds.

5

Resilience: Accepting And Overcoming Adversity

What is adversity?

Adversity refers to challenging circumstances or situations that one may face in life. These can include personal difficulties such as illness, loss, or financial troubles, as well as broader societal issues such as poverty, discrimination, or natural disasters. Adversity can take many forms and can range in severity, but it generally refers to any obstacle or problem that one must overcome. Adversity can test a person's strength and resilience and can present opportunities for personal growth and learning.

What is resilience?

Resilience refers to the ability to adapt and bounce back from adversity, challenges, and difficult situations. It involves the capacity to cope with stress and challenges, and to maintain or regain a sense of balance and well-being, even in the face of adversity. Resilience is important for mental and physical health, and it can be cultivated through various means such as having a positive mindset, social support, and developing coping strategies.

Examples of resilience include:

- A person who loses their job but quickly finds a new one and can maintain their financial stability.
- A person who goes through a divorce but can maintain healthy relationships and find happiness in the future.
- A person who is diagnosed with a chronic illness but can manage the condition and maintain a good quality of life.
- A community that is affected by a natural disaster but can come together and rebuild.
- A student who struggles academically but works hard and improves their grades.

Resilience is a crucial skill to have to lead a fulfilling life. The good news is that resilience is a skill that can be developed and strengthened. One of the key factors in building resilience is positive thinking. By maintaining an optimistic outlook, even in the face of difficult circumstances, we can better cope with adversity.

To build resilience, it's important to develop coping strategies, build a support system, and find meaning and purpose in adversity. Coping strategies can include things like exercise, mindfulness, or journaling. Building a support system can mean reaching out to friends and family, or seeking out a therapist or support group. For example, if you are going through a difficult time, you can build resilience by developing a daily exercise routine, reaching out to a friend to talk about your feelings, or finding a support group for people who are going through similar experiences.

Accepting adversity means acknowledging and facing the difficult situation, rather than denying or avoiding it. It's important to understand that adversity is a part of life and that everyone goes through difficult times. For example, if you have been diagnosed with a chronic illness, accepting it means acknowledging the reality of the situation and seeking out ways to manage the condition, rather than trying to ignore it or pretend it doesn't exist.

Overcoming adversity means taking action to overcome obstacles and challenges, setting and achieving goals, and using positive thinking to see opportunities in adversity. This can include things like seeking out professional help, making a plan to address the problem, and taking small, manageable steps to achieve your goals. For example, if you are dealing with a difficult personal problem, you can overcome it by seeking out therapy, setting a goal to address the problem, and taking small steps each day to work towards that goal.

Positive thinking helps us to maintain a sense of balance and well-being, even in the face of adversity.

When we think positively, we are more likely to see opportunities and solutions, rather than dwell on problems. For example, if you are going through a difficult time and find yourself thinking *"I'll never be able to handle this,"* a more positive thought would be *"I can handle this with time and effort, and I can ask for help when I need it."*

In conclusion, resilience is a crucial skill to have to lead a fulfilling life. Positive thinking plays a crucial role in building resilience, and it is important to accept and acknowledge difficult situations, build resilience and take action to overcome obstacles and challenges. Embrace the challenges and opportunities that come with adversity, and remember that resilience is a skill that can be developed and strengthened with practice.

10 things you can do today to practice resilience

- Practise gratitude by regularly writing down or sharing things you are thankful for.
- Prioritise self-care by setting aside time each day for

activities that make you feel good, such as exercise or meditation.
- Connect with others by reaching out to friends and family, or joining a support group or community organisation.
- Learn from challenges by reflecting on difficult experiences and identifying what you can learn from them.
- Set goals and work towards achieving them, as this can give you a sense of purpose and accomplishment.
- Practise mindfulness by paying attention to the present moment and being aware of your thoughts and feelings.
- Take a break when you need it, whether it's a short walk outside or a longer vacation.
- Learn to manage stress by identifying triggers and developing coping strategies.
- Get enough sleep, eat a healthy diet and exercise regularly.
- Practise forgiveness and let go of grudges, as holding onto negative feelings can harm your mental and physical well-being.

6

Positive Thinking And Mental Health

Positive thinking can have a powerful impact on our mental health. It can help us to cope with stress and adversity, improve our relationships, and lead a more fulfilling and happy life. However, many of us struggle with negative thoughts and self-doubt, which can lead to poor mental health and a decrease in overall well-being.

This chapter will explore the relationship between positive thinking and mental health, provide strategies for coping with negative thoughts, highlight behaviours to watch out for, and give practical tips for incorporating positive thinking into your daily life.

Understanding the impact of negative thinking on mental health

Negative thoughts and self-doubt can have a significant impact on our mental health. Research has shown that individuals who struggle with negative thoughts are more likely to develop mental health conditions such as depression and anxiety. Negative thoughts can also impact our daily functioning, leading to decreased motivation, difficulty concentrating, and a lack of enjoyment in activities that we once found pleasurable.

Some common negative thought patterns include catastrophising, in which we blow a minor issue out of proportion, and all-or-nothing thinking, in which we see things in black and white. For example, if you receive a low grade on a test, you might have a negative thought like *"I'm never going to pass this class,"* instead of a more realistic thought like *"I didn't do as well as I wanted on this test, but I can study more and do better next time."*

Strategies for coping with negative thoughts

One effective way to cope with negative thoughts is through cognitive-behavioural therapy (CBT). CBT is a form of therapy that helps individuals to identify and challenge negative thoughts and beliefs. Techniques such as reframing, in which you rephrase a negative thought more positively, and reality checking, in which you evaluate the evidence for and against a negative thought, can be extremely helpful in managing negative thoughts.

Another important aspect of coping with negative thoughts is learning to be kinder to yourself. This means practising self-compassion, which is the ability to treat yourself with the same kindness and understanding that you would offer to a friend. Instead of criticising yourself for having negative thoughts, try to acknowledge them and remind yourself that everyone has negative thoughts at times.

In addition to CBT and self-compassion, mindfulness practices such as meditation and deep breathing can also help to manage negative thoughts. Mindfulness is the practice of paying attention to the present moment and being aware of your thoughts and feelings. By becoming more mindful, you can learn to observe your negative thoughts without getting caught up in them.

Behaviours to watch out for

While it's normal to have negative thoughts at times, certain behaviours may indicate poor mental health. Warning signs to watch out for include social withdrawal, changes in appetite or sleep patterns, and self-harm. If you notice any of these behaviours in yourself or a loved one, it's important to seek professional help. You can speak to your primary care physician or find a therapist or support group in your area.

Easy ways to start improving today

One of the easiest ways to start incorporating positive thinking into your daily life is through the use of positive affirmations. Positive affirmations are statements that you repeat to yourself to counteract negative thoughts. For example, if you find yourself thinking *"I'm not good enough,"* you can counter that thought with the affirmation *"I am capable and strong."* Write down a list of positive affirmations that you can refer to when you need them.

Another way to improve your positive thinking is to focus on the present moment. Instead of dwelling on the past or worrying about the future, try to focus on the here and now. This can be done by engaging in activities that bring you joy and relaxation such as reading a book, listening to music, going for a walk in nature, or practising yoga.

Another tip for incorporating positive thinking into your daily life is to surround yourself with positivity. This means seeking out positive and supportive people in your life and limiting your exposure to negative news and social media.

You can also fill your living space with things that bring you joy, such as flowers, artwork, or photographs of loved ones.

Finally, it's important to build and maintain positive relationships with friends, family, and loved ones. Strong and supportive relationships can provide a sense of security and help counteract negative thoughts. You can do this by setting aside regular time to connect with loved ones, whether that's through phone calls, texts, or in-person visits.

Positive thinking can have a powerful impact on our mental health, helping us to cope with stress and adversity, improve our relationships, and lead a more fulfilling and happy life. By understanding the impact of negative thinking on mental health, learning strategies for coping with negative thoughts, being aware of behaviours to watch out for, and incorporating easy ways to start improving today, we can work towards developing a positive mindset.

Remember to be kind to yourself, take things one step at a time, and don't hesitate to seek professional help if needed.

7

Cognitive Behavioural Therapy And Positive Thinking

Cognitive Behavioural Therapy (CBT) is a type of therapy that focuses on changing negative thoughts and behaviours to promote positive thinking and well-being.

In this chapter, we will delve into the following topics:

The history of CBT: The origins and development of CBT, key figures in the history of CBT, such as Aaron Beck and Albert Ellis, and how CBT has evolved.

The Cognitive Model: Explanation of the cognitive model of CBT, how thoughts, feelings, and behaviours are interconnected, and the role of automatic thoughts and schemas in the cognitive model.

Techniques for promoting positive thinking: Identifying and challenging negative thoughts and beliefs, developing positive coping strategies, using cognitive restructuring and reframing techniques, and practising mindfulness and self-compassion.

Practical applications of CBT and positive thinking: How

CBT can be used to treat a variety of mental health conditions, such as depression and anxiety, how CBT can be used in daily life to promote positive thinking and well-being, and the role of therapy and self-help in CBT.

The history of CBT

Cognitive Behavioural Therapy (CBT) is a form of therapy that has been around for over 50 years. It was developed in the 1960s by Aaron Beck, a psychiatrist, and Albert Ellis, a psychologist. They observed that people often have negative thoughts and beliefs that contribute to their emotional and behavioural problems.

CBT has evolved, and it's now widely used in the treatment of various mental health conditions such as depression, anxiety, and PTSD. CBT is based on the idea that our thoughts, feelings, and behaviours are interconnected, and that by changing one, we can change the others.

The Cognitive Model

CBT is based on the cognitive model, which states that our thoughts, feelings, and behaviours are interconnected. The cognitive model proposes that our thoughts and beliefs influence our emotions and behaviours. For example, if you believe that you're not good enough, you may feel sad and unmotivated.

The cognitive model also recognises the role of automatic thoughts and schemas in our lives.

Automatic thoughts are the thoughts that come to mind without conscious effort. Schemas are underlying beliefs or assumptions about oneself and the world. These schemas can influence how we interpret events and can lead to negative thoughts and emotions if they are not accurate.

Techniques for promoting positive thinking

CBT offers a variety of techniques to promote positive thinking. One of the most important techniques is identifying and challenging negative thoughts and beliefs. This involves becoming aware of the automatic thoughts and schemas that are negative and not accurate and questioning them.

Another technique is developing positive coping strategies. These strategies can include things like exercise, mindfulness, or spending time with loved ones. These activities can help to reduce stress and improve mood.

Cognitive restructuring and reframing techniques are also key in CBT. These techniques involve challenging negative thoughts and beliefs and looking at things from a different perspective. For example, instead of saying *"I'll never be able to do this,"* reframe it to *"This is going to be difficult, but I know I can do it."* By reframing negative thoughts and beliefs, you can change the way you feel about a situation and improve your outlook on life.

Practical applications of CBT and positive thinking

The role of therapy and self-help in CBT is also important. Therapy can provide a safe and supportive space to explore and work on negative thoughts and beliefs. Self-help, on the other hand, can provide tools and techniques to work on these issues on your own. A combination of both therapy and self-help can be highly effective in promoting positive thinking and well-being.

The CBT principles

Catastrophising: This is a type of thinking where a person exaggerates the negative consequences of a situation. For example, if a person gets a minor injury and thinks *"I will never be able to walk again,"* instead of *"I may have a difficult recovery but I will get better."* To challenge this thinking, a person can remind themselves of past situations where they faced challenges and overcame them, and also remind themselves that they have a support system to help them.

Black and white thinking: This is a type of thinking where a person sees things in absolutes, such as "good" or "bad" instead of a more nuanced approach.]To challenge this thinking, a person can remind themselves of past successes and remind themselves that one situation does not define them.

Negative self-talk: This is when a person speaks to themselves in a negative way, such as *"I'm not good enough"* or *"I'll never be successful."* For example, if a person is interviewing for a job and thinks *"I am not qualified for this job"* instead of *"I may not have all the qualifications, but I have skills and experiences that can contribute to this job."* To challenge this thinking, a person can remind themselves of their strengths and past successes, and remind themselves that they deserve the opportunity to interview for the job.

Automatic thoughts: These are thoughts that pop into a person's mind without them being aware of it. They can be positive or negative and they can influence how a person feels and acts. For example, if a person is going to an event and their automatic thought is *"nobody will like me"* instead of *"I may not know everyone at the event, but I can make new connections."* To challenge this thinking, a person can remind themselves that they can make friends and that people are generally friendly and open to meeting new people.

Setting and achieving goals: CBT encourages setting specific, measurable, and realistic goals and taking steps to achieve them. For example, if a person wants to improve their physical fitness, they can set a goal to exercise for 30 minutes three times a week, and create a plan to achieve that goal by setting a schedule, finding a workout buddy, or joining a fitness class.

The practice of mindfulness: CBT encourages practising mindfulness. For example, if a person is feeling anxious about a future event, they can practice mindfulness by paying attention to the present moment and focusing on their breath, rather than worrying about the future.

Action-taking: CBT involves taking action and working towards goals in addition to positive thinking. For example, if a person wants to improve their relationship with their partner, they can set a goal to communicate more effectively, and take action by scheduling regular check-ins with their partner, learning active listening skills, or seeking couple's therapy.

What you can start doing today

Identifying and challenging negative thoughts: One of the most basic CBT exercises is to identify and challenge negative thoughts. This can be done by keeping a thought diary, where you write down any negative thoughts that come to mind throughout the day. Once you have identified them, you can challenge them by asking yourself if they are based on facts or assumptions, and if there is any evidence to support them.

Cognitive restructuring: Another CBT exercise is cognitive restructuring, which involves changing the way you think about a situation. For example, if you find yourself having negative thoughts about a situation, try to reframe them more positively. Instead of thinking *"I'm going to fail,"* think *"I'm going to do my best."*

Mindfulness meditation: Mindfulness meditation is a CBT exercise that involves paying attention to the present moment, without judgment. This can be done by focusing on your breath, or by paying attention to the sensations in your body.

Gratitude journaling: Gratitude journaling is a CBT exercise that involves writing down things you are grateful for each day. This can help to shift your focus from negative thoughts and feelings to positive ones.

Problem-solving: CBT also includes problem-solving techniques, that involve breaking down a problem into smaller parts and identifying potential solutions.

Visualisation: Visualisation is a CBT exercise that involves creating mental images of yourself achieving your goals. This can help to activate the same parts of the brain as when you do the task, making it more likely to happen.

Time management: CBT also includes time management techniques, that involve breaking down your day into smaller tasks, prioritising, and setting short and long-term goals.

It's important to keep in mind that CBT exercises take time and practice to master.

Where can you get CBT treatment?

Cognitive Behavioural Therapy (CBT) treatment can be obtained from a variety of sources, including:

Mental health clinics or hospitals: Many clinics and hospitals offer CBT treatment, usually provided by licenced mental health professionals such as psychologists, psychiatrists, and licenced clinical social workers.

Private therapists and counsellors: Private therapists and counsellors who specialise in CBT can provide treatment on an individual basis. They may have a private practice or work in a group practice.

Employee assistance programs (EAPs): Many employers offer employee assistance programs that provide short-term counselling, including CBT, to employees free of charge.

Community health centres: Community health centres may offer CBT treatment, often at a reduced cost or on a sliding scale based on income.

Online and mobile apps: Some online and mobile apps provide CBT treatment, such as guided meditations, self-help tools, and interactive activities.

Universities and colleges: Some universities and colleges offer CBT treatment through their counselling centres or psychology clinics, often provided by graduate students under the supervision of licenced professionals.

It's important to note that not all providers of CBT are licenced or qualified to provide this type of treatment, so it's advisable to check the credentials of the therapist or counsellor before starting treatment.

CBT is a powerful tool for promoting positive thinking and well-being. By identifying and challenging negative thoughts and beliefs, developing positive coping strategies, using cognitive restructuring and reframing techniques, practising mindfulness and self-compassion, and seeking therapy and self-help, you can improve your outlook on life and reduce stress.

As you continue on your journey towards positive thinking and well-being, remember to be kind and understanding with yourself, celebrate your successes and seek support when needed.

8

Positive Thinking And Success

In this chapter, we will explore the connection between positive thinking and success, and provide an overview of the chapter, including definitions, myths, strategies, tips, and feelings. We will also provide real-life examples and strategies for women.

Positive thinking is the act of focusing on the good things in life and working towards a positive outcome.

Success, on the other hand, can mean different things to different people. It can be achieving a specific goal, such as getting a promotion at work or starting a business, or it can be more general, such as feeling fulfilled and happy.

Regardless of what success means to you, it's important to understand that positive thinking plays a crucial role in achieving it.

In this chapter, we will delve into the following topics:

Defining success: Personal definition of success and how it differs from person to person, the importance of setting specific and measurable goals, and recognising and valuing different forms of success.

Myths about positive thinking and success: Dispelling the myth that positive thinking alone leads to success, the importance of taking action and working towards goals in addition to positive thinking, and understanding the difference between positive thinking and unrealistic optimism.

Strategies for incorporating positive thinking into goal-setting and action-taking: Techniques for setting and achieving goals, such as SMART goals and visualisation, the power of positive affirmations and self-talk, mindfulness practices for staying present and focused on the task at hand, the importance of self-compassion and being kind to oneself during the process of reaching goals.

Tips for overcoming obstacles and staying positive: Identifying and reframing negative thoughts and limiting beliefs, building a support system and seeking help when needed, finding inspiration and motivation through role models and success stories, practising resilience and learning from failure.

Defining success

Success means different things to different people. For some, it's about achieving a specific goal, such as getting a promotion at work or starting a business. For others, it's about feeling fulfilled and happy. Regardless of what success means to you, it's important to understand that positive thinking plays a crucial role in achieving it.

When defining success, it's important to set specific and measurable goals. For example, instead of saying "I want to be successful," say "I want to start my own business and make $100,000 in revenue in the first year." This specific and measurable goal is more likely to be achieved than a general one.

It's also important to recognise and value different forms of success. For example, success doesn't always have to be financial. It can be emotional, such as finding inner peace, or social, such as building strong relationships.

Myths about positive thinking and success

One of the biggest myths about positive thinking and success is that positive thinking alone leads to success. This is not true. Positive thinking is an important part of the process, but it's not the only thing. You also need to take action and work towards your goals.

Another myth is that positive thinking leads to unrealistic optimism. While it's important to have a positive attitude, it's also important to be realistic and understand that there will be obstacles along the way. Positive thinking helps you to overcome these obstacles and stay motivated, but it doesn't mean that everything will be easy.

Strategies for incorporating positive thinking into goal-setting and action-taking

There are several strategies for incorporating positive thinking into goal-setting and action-taking. One of the most effective techniques is setting SMART goals, which stands for Specific, Measurable, Achievable, Relevant, and Time-bound. By setting SMART goals, you are more likely to achieve them because they are clear and attainable.

Visualisation is another powerful strategy for incorporating positive thinking into goal-setting and action-taking. By visualising yourself achieving your goal, you are more likely to make it a reality. This is because visualisation helps to activate the same parts of the brain as when you do the task.

Positive affirmations and self-talk are also effective strategies for incorporating positive thinking. Positive affirmations are short, powerful statements that you repeat to yourself to help change your mindset. For example, instead of saying "I can't do this," say "I am capable and strong." Self-talk is the internal dialogue you have with yourself. By being mindful of your self-talk and making sure it is positive, you are more likely to achieve your goals.

Mindfulness practices, such as meditation, can also help you stay present and focused on the task at hand. By being present and not dwelling on the past or worrying about the future, you can stay focused and motivated to achieve your goals.

In addition to all of these strategies, it's important to practice self-compassion and be kind to yourself during the process of reaching your goals. This means being gentle and understanding with yourself when things don't go as planned, and celebrating your successes along the way.

Tips for overcoming obstacles and staying positive

Obstacles are a natural part of the journey to success, but it's important to not let them defeat you. One way to overcome obstacles is by identifying and reframing negative thoughts and limiting beliefs. For example, instead of thinking "I'll never be able to do this," reframe it to "This is going to be difficult, but I know I can do it."

Another tip for overcoming obstacles is to build a support system and seek help when needed. Having people in your life who believe in you and support you can make all the difference.

Inspiration and motivation can also be found through role models and success stories. Look to people who have achieved what you want to achieve and learn from their experiences.

Finally, practising resilience and learning from failure is crucial. It's important to understand that failure is not the end, but rather an opportunity to learn and grow.

Positive thinking is an essential part of achieving success, and by incorporating positive thinking into goal-setting and action-taking, you can achieve your goals.

It's important to set specific and measurable goals, recognise and value different forms of success, and practice self-compassion and kindness towards yourself.

Remember, obstacles will inevitably arise, but by identifying and reframing negative thoughts, building a support system, finding inspiration and motivation, practising resilience and learning from failure, you can overcome them and stay positive.

As you continue on your journey towards success, keep in mind the importance of a positive mindset and remember to celebrate your successes along the way.

9

The Importance Of Mindfulness And Meditation On Positive Thinking

In this chapter, we will explore how mindfulness and meditation can improve positive thinking, and provide an overview of the chapter, including the history and benefits of mindfulness and meditation, practical tips and strategies, and real-life examples.

Mindfulness and meditation are practices that involve paying attention to the present moment and being aware of your thoughts, feelings, and surroundings. These practices have been around for thousands of years and have been used in a variety of cultures and traditions.

In recent years, there has been a growing body of scientific research that has shown the benefits of mindfulness and meditation for mental and physical health. Studies have found that mindfulness and meditation can reduce stress, anxiety and depression, and improve emotional regulation.

In this chapter, we will delve into the following topics:

The history of mindfulness and meditation: The origins and development of mindfulness and meditation, key figures in the history of mindfulness and meditation, such as Jon Kabat-Zinn and Pema Chodron, and how mindfulness and meditation have evolved.

The benefits of mindfulness and meditation: Explanation of the scientific research behind the benefits of mindfulness and meditation, how mindfulness and meditation can improve mental and physical health, such as reducing stress, anxiety, and depression, and improve emotional regulation.

We will also discuss the benefits of mindfulness and meditation for women specifically, such as reducing feelings of isolation and anxiety in motherhood.

Practical tips and strategies for incorporating mindfulness and meditation into daily life: Techniques for getting started with mindfulness and meditation, tips for creating a mindfulness and meditation practice that works for you, such as finding a quiet space and setting aside time each day, strategies for incorporating mindfulness and meditation into daily activities, such as walking, cooking, and interacting with others.

The history of mindfulness and meditation

Mindfulness and meditation have been around for thousands of years and have been used in a variety of cultures and traditions.

The origins of mindfulness can be traced back to Eastern religious and spiritual practices, such as Buddhism and Hinduism. In the West, mindfulness was popularised by figures like Jon Kabat-Zinn, who developed the Mindfulness-Based Stress Reduction (MBSR) program in the 1970s. This program has been used to treat a variety of mental and physical health conditions and has been widely studied and researched.

Pema Chodron, an American Buddhist nun, has also been instrumental in popularising mindfulness and meditation in the West. She has written numerous books on the topic and has taught mindfulness and meditation to thousands of people.

The benefits of mindfulness and meditation

There is a growing body of scientific research that has shown the benefits of mindfulness and meditation for mental and physical health. Studies have found that mindfulness and meditation can reduce stress, anxiety, and depression, and improve emotional regulation.

Mindfulness and meditation have also been found to have many specific benefits for women. For example, studies have shown that mindfulness and meditation can reduce feelings of isolation and anxiety in motherhood. Mindfulness and meditation can also help women to cope with menopause and other life transitions.

Practical tips and strategies for incorporating mindfulness and meditation into daily life

Getting started with mindfulness and meditation can be intimidating, but it doesn't have to be. There are a variety of techniques and strategies that can help to make mindfulness and meditation more accessible and manageable.

One of the simplest ways to get started with mindfulness and meditation is to try guided meditation. There are many free guided meditations available online, or you can use a meditation app like Headspace or Calm.

Another way to make mindfulness and meditation more manageable is to incorporate them into your daily activities. For example, you can practice mindfulness while you're cooking, walking, or even doing the dishes.

Questions and answers

Q. What is mindfulness?

A. Mindfulness is the practice of being present and aware of your thoughts, feelings, and surroundings at the moment. It involves paying attention to your breath and the sensations in your body and observing your thoughts and feelings without judgment.

Q. What is meditation?

A. Meditation is a practice that involves focusing your mind on a particular object, thought, or activity to achieve a mentally clear and emotionally calm state. It can involve a variety of techniques such as concentration, visualisation, and mindfulness.

Q. What are the benefits of mindfulness and meditation?

A. Research has shown that mindfulness and meditation can have a variety of benefits for mental and physical health, such as reducing stress, anxiety, and depression, and improve emotional regulation, improving sleep, reducing chronic pain, and even reducing blood pressure.

Q. How do I start a mindfulness and meditation practice?

A. Starting a mindfulness and meditation practice can be as simple as setting aside a few minutes each day to focus on your breath and the present moment. You can also try guided meditations or mindfulness exercises, or take a class or workshop to learn more about the practice.

Q. How often should I practice mindfulness and meditation?

A. The frequency of mindfulness and meditation practice can vary from person to person. It's generally recommended to start with a few minutes a day and gradually increase the time as you feel comfortable.

Q. Can I practice mindfulness and meditation anywhere?

A. Yes, you can practice mindfulness and meditation anywhere and at any time. You can practice mindfulness and meditation in a quiet room, in nature, or even while walking or standing in line.

Q. How do mindfulness and meditation affect the brain?

A. Research has shown that mindfulness and meditation can change the structure and function of the brain, particularly in areas associated with stress, emotion regulation, and attention. It has also been found to increase the size of the hippocampus, the part of the brain responsible for learning and memory.

Q. Can mindfulness and meditation replace traditional therapy?

A. Mindfulness and meditation can be effective complementary treatment for many mental health conditions, but it is not intended to replace traditional therapy or medication. Always consult with a mental health professional to determine the best course of treatment for you.

Q. How long does it take to see the benefits of mindfulness and meditation?

A. It can take time and regular practice to see the benefits of mindfulness and meditation. Some people may notice positive changes within a few days or weeks, while for others it may take longer. It's important to be consistent with your practice and to be patient with yourself as you build your mindfulness and meditation skills. It's also important to keep in mind that the benefits of mindfulness and meditation can be cumulative, so the more you practice, the more benefits you may experience over time.

Here is an example of a guided meditation script:

- Begin by finding a comfortable seated position, with your back straight and your feet firmly planted on the ground.
- Close your eyes and take a deep breath in through your nose and out through your mouth.
- Take another deep breath in and out, and as you exhale, allow your body to relax.
- Bring your attention to your breath, noticing the sensation of the air entering and leaving your body.
- Let your breath be natural and easy, without trying to change it in any way.
- As you focus on your breath, you may notice that your mind starts to wander. When this happens, simply acknowledge the thoughts and gently guide your attention back to your breath.
- As you continue to focus on your breath, you may notice your body becoming more and more relaxed.
- Bring to mind a peaceful place, it can be a real place or an imagined one, somewhere you feel calm, safe and at peace.
- Imagine yourself in this place, using all your senses to take in the sights, sounds, and feelings of this place.
- Stay in this peaceful place for as long as you like, allowing yourself to fully relax and let go of any tension or stress.
- When you're ready, slowly open your eyes and take a deep breath in and out.
- Take a moment to notice how you feel and bring that feeling of calm and peace with you as you go about your day.

You can adapt this script to your liking, and add different elements like a focus on gratitude, self-compassion or a positive affirmation.

Mindfulness and meditation are powerful tools that can help to reduce stress, anxiety, and depression, and improve emotional regulation. By incorporating mindfulness and meditation into daily life, women can improve their positive thinking and overall well-being.

Remember to be kind and understanding with yourself, celebrate your successes and seek support when needed. And, always keep in mind that mindfulness and meditation take time and practice to master.

10

Practising Gratitude And Appreciation

Gratitude and appreciation are two powerful emotions that can positively impact our mental, physical, and emotional well-being. They are closely related, with gratitude being the feeling of thankfulness for what we have and appreciate being the recognition of the value and worth of something or someone. Practising gratitude and appreciation can be a simple yet effective way to improve our overall happiness and satisfaction with life.

Understanding the benefits of gratitude and appreciation

Research has shown that practising gratitude and appreciation can have a wide range of benefits for our mental and physical health. These benefits include:

Improved mood and emotional well-being: Gratitude and appreciation can help to reduce feelings of stress, anxiety, and depression. By focusing on the positive aspects of our lives, we can shift our attention away from negative thoughts and emotions.

Increased resilience and coping skills: Practising gratitude and appreciation can help us to develop a more resilient mindset, which can be especially useful during difficult times. It can also help us to better cope with stress and adversity.

Improved relationships: Expressing gratitude and appreciation to others can strengthen relationships and improve communication. It can also increase feelings of connection and social support.

Better physical health: Gratitude and appreciation have been linked to improved sleep, reduced pain, and a stronger immune system.

Actionable steps for practising gratitude and appreciation

Keeping a gratitude journal: One of the simplest and most effective ways to practise gratitude is to keep a gratitude journal. Set aside some time each day, such as before going to bed or first thing in the morning, to write down a few things that you are grateful for. This can be anything from small things like a delicious meal or a warm blanket to bigger things like good health or a loving family.

Writing thank-you notes: Another way to express gratitude is to write thank-you notes to people who have made a positive impact on your life. This could be a friend, family member, teacher, or even a stranger who has helped you in some way. Take the time to think about why you are grateful for this person and what they have done for you.

Expressing appreciation in person or through other forms of communication: In addition to writing thank-you notes, make a point to express gratitude and appreciation to people in your life regularly. This could be through verbal communication, such as telling someone how much you appreciate them or how much their friendship means to you. It could also be through nonverbal communication, such as giving a hug or a smile.

Incorporating gratitude and appreciation into daily routines and practices: Make gratitude and appreciation a part of your daily routine by setting reminders or triggers throughout the day. For example, you could set a reminder on your phone to take a moment and be grateful for something specific at a certain time of day. Or, you could make a habit of expressing gratitude before or after a meal.

Practising mindfulness and being present in the moment: Mindfulness is the practice of being present and fully engaged in the moment. It can be helpful to take a few minutes each day to be mindful and fully engage in an activity or experience. This can help you to be more aware of the things you have to be grateful for and to appreciate the present moment.

Starting today

Starting to practise gratitude and appreciation doesn't have to be complicated or time-consuming. Here are a few easy and practical ways to get started:

- Choose one or two of the actionable steps listed above and commit to incorporating them into your daily routine.
- Make a conscious effort to notice and acknowledge the small things in life that you are grateful for.
- Challenge yourself to express gratitude and appreciation to at least one person every day.
- Remember that it takes time and consistency to make gratitude and appreciation a habit.
- Be patient with yourself and keep trying, even if you slip up or forget.

It's important to remember that practising gratitude and appreciation is not about being happy all the time, ignoring problems or pretending everything is perfect. It's about shifting our focus to the positive things in our lives and being mindful of the things we have to be grateful for, even in difficult times.

It takes time and effort to make gratitude and appreciation a regular part of our lives, but the benefits are well worth it.

In conclusion, practising gratitude and appreciation can be a powerful tool for improving our overall well-being.

By making a conscious effort to focus on the positive aspects of our lives, we can shift our attention away from negative thoughts and emotions, and improve our mood, emotional well-being, relationships, and physical health. So start today, and make gratitude and appreciation a regular part of your daily routine.

11

Positive Thinking And Building Relationships

Positive thinking plays a crucial role in building and maintaining healthy relationships. It is a mindset that allows individuals to focus on the good in themselves and others, rather than dwelling on negative thoughts and feelings. When we adopt a positive attitude towards ourselves and others, we are more likely to build stronger and more meaningful connections with the people around us.

In this chapter, we will explore the various aspects of positive thinking in relationships. We will begin by defining what positive thinking means in the context of relationships and how it can differ from person to person. Next, we will discuss the importance of setting specific and measurable goals for building relationships. We will also examine some common myths about positive thinking and building relationships, and explore strategies for incorporating positive thinking into building and maintaining relationships. Finally, we will provide tips for overcoming obstacles and staying positive in relationships, as well as answer some common questions and challenges that women may face when building positive relationships.

Defining positive thinking in relationships

Personal definition of positive thinking in relationships and how it differs from person to person:

Positive thinking in relationships can be defined as an attitude or mindset that focuses on the good in ourselves and others. It involves seeing the best in people, even during difficult times, and focusing on the positive aspects of a relationship rather than dwelling on negative thoughts and feelings. The way that positive thinking is expressed in relationships can differ from person to person, but ultimately it is about finding the good in others and looking for ways to build and strengthen connections.

The importance of setting specific and measurable goals for building relationships: Setting specific and measurable goals is essential for building and maintaining healthy relationships. By setting clear and achievable goals, you can focus your efforts on what you want to achieve in your relationships, and measure your progress over time. For example, you might set a goal to have regular check-ins with a friend or to make an effort to listen more actively in conversations with your partner. By setting goals, you can work towards building stronger and more meaningful connections with the people in your life.

Recognising and valuing different forms of positive thinking in relationships: There are many different forms of positive thinking in relationships, and it is important to recognise and value the different ways that people express positivity. For example, some people may express positivity through words of encouragement and support, while others may do so through acts of kindness and generosity. By recognising and valuing the different forms of positive thinking in relationships, we can learn to appreciate and build stronger connections with the people in our lives.

Myths about positive thinking and building relationships

Dispelling the myth that positive thinking alone leads to successful relationships:

Many people believe that if they just think positively, their relationships will be successful. However, this is not the case. Positive thinking is just one aspect of building and maintaining healthy relationships. Communication, compromise, and empathy are also essential for building successful relationships. By focusing on these key areas, along with positive thinking, you can build stronger and more meaningful connections with the people in your life.

The importance of communication, compromise, and empathy in addition to positive thinking: Communication is key to building and maintaining healthy relationships. It is essential to be able to express your thoughts and feelings clearly and effectively and to be able to listen actively to others. Compromise is also essential for building successful relationships. It is important to be able to find common ground and to be willing to make sacrifices.

Understanding the difference between positive thinking and unrealistic optimism in relationships: Positive thinking and unrealistic optimism are not the same things. Positive thinking involves seeing the best in people, even during difficult times, and focusing on the positive aspects of a relationship. Unrealistic optimism, on the other hand, is when you believe that things will always turn out well, regardless of the circumstances. This can lead to disappointment and frustration when things don't go as planned. It is important to find a balance between positive thinking and realistic optimism in relationships so that you can build strong connections with others without setting yourself up for disappointment.

Strategies for incorporating positive thinking into building and maintaining relationships

Techniques for effective communication and active listening: Effective communication and active listening are essential for building and maintaining healthy relationships. When communicating, it is important to use "I" statements to express your thoughts and feelings, rather than blaming or accusing the other person. Active listening, on the other hand, involves fully listening to and understanding the other person's thoughts and feelings, rather than just waiting for your turn to speak.

The power of positive affirmations and self-talk in relationships: Positive affirmations and self-talk can be powerful tools for building and maintaining healthy relationships. Positive affirmations are statements that help to change negative thoughts and beliefs into positive ones. For example, instead of saying "I'm not good enough", you can say "I am worthy and deserving of love and respect". Self-talk, on the other hand, is the constant dialogue that goes on in your mind. By paying attention to your self-talk and reframing negative thoughts, you can build a more positive mindset in your relationships.

Mindfulness practices for staying present and focused on the relationship: Mindfulness practices, such as meditation and yoga, can help you to stay present and focused on your relationships. By being present in the moment, you can fully engage with the other person and build stronger connections. Mindfulness practices can also help you to be more aware of your thoughts and feelings, and to manage them more effectively.

The importance of self-compassion and being kind to oneself during conflicts or challenges in relationships: Self-compassion is essential for building and maintaining healthy relationships. It involves being kind and understanding towards yourself, even during conflicts or challenges. When we are compassionate towards ourselves, we are better able to handle difficult situations in relationships and to communicate and connect with others more positively.

Tips for overcoming obstacles and staying positive in relationships

Identifying and reframing negative thoughts and limiting beliefs about relationships: Negative thoughts and limiting beliefs can hold us back in relationships. By identifying and reframing these thoughts and beliefs, we can build a more positive mindset and overcome obstacles in our relationships. For example, instead of thinking "I will never find someone who truly loves me", you can reframe that thought to "I am worthy of love and I will continue to work on building healthy relationships".

Building a support system and seeking help when needed, such as therapy or counselling: Building a support system and seeking help when needed are essential for overcoming obstacles and staying positive in relationships. A support system can provide you with the emotional and practical support you need to navigate difficult situations in relationships. Therapy or counselling can also help you to work through any issues you may be facing and to develop new coping strategies.

Finding inspiration and motivation through role models and success stories of healthy relationships: Finding inspiration and motivation through role models and success stories of healthy relationships can help you to stay positive and motivated in your relationships. Seeing the positive examples of others can remind you that healthy relationships are possible and give you hope for your relationships. You can find inspiration and motivation through reading books, watching movies or documentaries, or even talking to friends or family members who have healthy relationships.

Practising resilience and learning from past relationship challenges: Resilience is the ability to bounce back from challenges and adversity. By practising resilience, you can learn from past relationship challenges and use that knowledge to build stronger and more positive relationships in the future. This may involve reflecting on past challenges, identifying what went wrong, and learning from it. It can also involve developing new coping strategies and building a support system to help you navigate any future challenges.

Common questions and challenges in building positive relationships

How to handle difficult conversations and conflicts in relationships: Difficult conversations and conflicts are a natural part of any relationship. To handle them effectively, it is important to approach them with a positive attitude and to use effective communication techniques, such as active listening and "I" statements. It is also important to stay calm, take a break if necessary, and come back to the conversation later if needed.

How to deal with trust issues and past hurt in relationships: Trust issues and past hurt can be challenging to deal with in relationships. To overcome these challenges, it is important to communicate openly and honestly with your partner and to work together to rebuild trust. You may also find it helpful to seek the help of a therapist or counsellor, who can help you to work through any past hurt and build a more positive and healthy relationship.

How to build and maintain healthy boundaries in relationships: Building and maintaining healthy boundaries is essential for building positive relationships. Healthy boundaries involve setting limits on what is acceptable and what is not, and communicating these limits to your partner. This may involve setting limits on time spent with friends and family or setting boundaries around personal space and privacy. It is important to build and maintain healthy boundaries in relationships to maintain respect and trust in the relationship.

12

Practical Ways To Make Your Relationship More Positive:

Here are some practical ways to help make your relationship more positive:

Practise gratitude: Take time every day to express gratitude for the positive aspects of your relationship. This can be done through verbal or written expressions of gratitude, or small gestures of appreciation.

Communicate openly and honestly: Regularly communicate with your partner about your thoughts, feelings, and needs. This will help to build trust and understanding in the relationship.

Show acts of kindness: Small acts of kindness can go a long way in making a relationship more positive. These can include things like cooking a meal for your partner, doing a household chore for them, or leaving a heartfelt note.

Spend quality time together: Make time for activities that you both enjoy, and focus on being present and engaged in the moment. This will help to strengthen the bond between you and your partner.

Practise forgiveness: Forgiveness is key to building positive relationships. Learn to let go of grudges and resentments, and focus on moving forward in a positive direction.

Show affection: Showing physical affection such as hugging, holding hands, and kissing can help to build emotional intimacy and strengthen the connection in the relationship.

Seek help when needed: If you are facing challenges in your relationship, don't hesitate to seek help from a therapist or counsellor. They can provide you with the support and guidance you need to navigate difficult situations and build a more positive relationship.

Be open to change: Be open to learning and growing in the relationship. Be willing to change your behaviour and perspective when needed, to improve the relationship.

Practise empathy: Try to put yourself in your partner's shoes and understand their perspective. This will help to build empathy and understanding in the relationship.

Show appreciation: Show appreciation for your partner's positive qualities and for the things they do for you. This will help to build mutual respect and strengthen the relationship.

Building positive relationships takes time and effort. It is important to continue working on incorporating positive thinking into your relationships and to seek support when needed. By following the strategies and tips outlined in this chapter, and by seeking the help of a therapist or counsellor when needed, you can build stronger and more positive relationships with the people in your relationships and seek support when needed.

It is normal to face challenges and obstacles in relationships, but with a positive mindset and the right strategies and support, you can overcome them and build stronger, more positive connections with the people in your life.

Remember to be kind and compassionate towards yourself, and to take the time to reflect on your progress and celebrate your successes. Keep in mind that building positive relationships is a continuous journey, and with the right mindset and approach, you can achieve the fulfilling relationships that you desire.

13

The Dangers Of Negative Thinking

Negative thinking can have a significant impact on our physical and psychological health. It can lead to an increased risk of chronic diseases, negatively affect the immune system, and impact our sleep and overall physical well-being. Additionally, negative thinking can increase the risk of mental health issues such as anxiety and depression and harm self-esteem and self-worth, as well as relationships and social interactions. In this chapter, we will delve into the causes, effects, and strategies for managing negative thinking.

Defining negative thinking

Negative thinking can take on many forms, and it can look different for everyone. It can manifest as negative self-talk, negative assumptions, or even constant worrying.

Negative thinking refers to thoughts and attitudes that are characterised by a negative outlook on life. These thoughts can take many forms, such as catastrophising, black-and-white thinking, and negative self-talk. It's important to recognise and identify negative thoughts to effectively overcome them.

Understanding the root cause of negative thinking

Negative thinking can have many underlying causes such as past experiences, traumatic events, and learned patterns.
Research has shown that childhood experiences, particularly those involving neglect or abuse, can have a significant impact on the development of negative thinking patterns in adulthood.

Our parents or caregivers play a big role in shaping our thoughts and beliefs about ourselves and the world around us. Studies have also found that emotional neglect or verbal abuse from parents can have a long-term impact on an individual's cognitive and emotional development.

Emotions and stress can also play a role in negative thinking. To effectively overcome negative thoughts, it's important to address the root cause of these thoughts. This may include seeking therapy or counselling to process past experiences and learn coping mechanisms.

The importance of identifying and understanding negative thought patterns: Negative thoughts can easily become a habit and it's important to be aware of them, so you can take steps to change them. Understanding the triggers that lead to negative thoughts can help you to identify and manage them more effectively.

The connection between negative thinking and stress, anxiety, and depression: Negative thinking can contribute to the development of stress, anxiety, and depression. When negative thoughts become overwhelming, they can lead to feelings of hopelessness and helplessness, which can contribute to the development of these mental health conditions.

Causes of negative thinking

Trauma, past experiences, and learned behaviours: Past experiences, particularly traumatic ones, can have a significant impact on our thoughts and behaviours. Trauma can lead to negative thought patterns, such as feeling unsafe or unworthy, that can be difficult to overcome without professional help.

Social and cultural influences: The way we perceive the world around us is often shaped by our social and cultural environment. Negative messages in the media and society can lead to negative thoughts and beliefs about ourselves and others.

Biological and genetic factors: Research has shown that there may be a genetic component to negative thinking. Some individuals may be more prone to negative thinking due to their biology and genetics.

Physical effects of negative thinking

Negative thinking can also have negative effects on physical health. Chronic stress and anxiety caused by negative thinking can lead to a variety of physical symptoms such as headaches, muscle tension, and stomach problems. It can also weaken the immune system, making a person more susceptible to illness.

Increased risk of chronic diseases: Negative thinking has been linked to a greater risk of chronic diseases such as heart disease and diabetes. Negative thoughts and emotions can trigger the release of stress hormones, which can lead to inflammation in the body, contributing to the development of these diseases.

Negative impact on immune system function: Negative thoughts and emotions can also harm the immune system. Chronic stress and anxiety can lead to a suppression of the immune system, making it less able to fight off infections and illnesses.

Negative impact on sleep and overall physical well-being: Negative thoughts can also affect our sleep, leading to insomnia and other sleep-related problems. Lack of sleep can further contribute to negative thoughts and feelings, making it difficult to break the cycle.

Psychological effects of negative thinking

Increased risk of mental health issues, such as anxiety and depression: Negative thinking can increase the risk of mental health issues, particularly anxiety and depression. Negative thoughts can lead to feelings of hopelessness and helplessness, which can contribute to the development of these conditions.

Impaired decision-making: Negative thinking can also impair decision-making abilities. Negative thoughts can cloud judgment and make it difficult to see things objectively, leading to poor decision-making.

Decreased motivation and productivity: Negative thinking can also lead to decreased motivation and productivity. Negative thoughts can make it difficult to focus and stay motivated, leading to decreased productivity and a lack of accomplishment.

Poor relationships: Negative thinking can also harm relationships. Negative thoughts and attitudes can lead to conflicts and misunderstandings, making it difficult to build and maintain healthy relationships.

Inability to cope with stress: Negative thinking can also make it difficult for a person to cope with stress. Negative thoughts can lead to feelings of hopelessness and helplessness, making it difficult to find solutions to problems and healthily deal with stress.

It's important to note that negative thinking is a common human experience and can be overcome with the right approach and help. Identifying negative thoughts and patterns, challenging them, and replacing them with more positive and realistic thoughts are some of the ways to overcome negative thinking.

14

Understanding Negative People - And How To Avoid Them

Negative people can have a significant impact on our mental and physical health. They can drain our energy, bring us down, and even lead to the development of mental health issues such as anxiety and depression. To improve our overall well-being, it's important to understand and avoid negative people.

In this chapter, we will discuss strategies for understanding, identifying, and avoiding negative people. We'll also explore the underlying causes of negative behaviour, offer tips for maintaining a positive mindset, and address common questions and challenges that women may face regarding negative people.

Defining negative people

Negative people are individuals who tend to have a negative outlook on life. They can take many forms, such as energy drainers, gossipers, and complainers. They can be anyone from co-workers, friends, or even family members. It's important to recognise and identify negative people to effectively avoid them.

Understanding the root cause of negative behaviour:
Negative behaviour can have many underlying causes such as past experiences, traumatic events, and learned patterns. Research has shown that childhood experiences can have a significant impact on the development of negative behaviour patterns in adulthood. Negative behaviour can also be a result of the emotional stress that an individual may be going through. To effectively avoid and deal with negative people, it's important to understand the root cause of their negative behaviour.

Strategies for avoiding negative people: Several techniques can be used to identify and avoid negative people. One of the most effective techniques is setting boundaries and limiting interactions with negative people. Positive self-talk and affirmations can also help maintain a positive mindset. Mindfulness practices such as meditation and focusing on the present moment can also help become more aware of negative people in your environment. It is also important to practice self-compassion and be kind to oneself during the process of avoiding negative people.

Common questions and challenges

Q. How do we handle negative/toxic people in the workplace or close relationships?

A. This can be achieved by setting boundaries, limiting interactions and communicating effectively. Dealing with toxic family members or friends can be a tricky situation. However, it's important to remember that you have the right to surround yourself with people who support and uplift you. In these situations, setting boundaries and limiting interactions may be necessary.

Q. How can I protect myself from toxic people?

A. Setting healthy boundaries, learning to say no, and limiting contact with toxic people can help protect yourself from their negative effects. You can also try to focus on self-care and surround yourself with positive, supportive people.

Q. What can I do if I'm in a relationship with a toxic person?

A. It's important to seek help from a professional therapist or counsellor if you are in a relationship with a toxic person. They can help you to identify and address the toxic behaviour, and develop strategies for coping and setting boundaries.

Q. How can I help a friend or family member who is in a toxic relationship?

A. Supporting a friend or family member in a toxic relationship can be difficult, but it's important to be a good listener, offer support, and encourage them to seek help from a professional therapist or counsellor.

Q. How can I deal with a toxic co-worker?

A. Setting boundaries, focusing on your tasks, and avoiding unnecessary interactions with toxic co-workers can help to minimise their negative impact on your work environment.

Q. Can toxic people change?

A. Some toxic people may be willing to change, but it's important to remember that change is a difficult and ongoing process. It's important to focus on your well-being and not to enable or enable toxic behaviour.

Q. What are some red flags that someone might be toxic?

A. Some red flags that someone might be toxic include manipulation, control, lack of empathy, and a tendency to blame others for their problems.

Additionally, it's important to acknowledge that it's not always possible to avoid negative people completely, and it's okay to take time for yourself and practise self-care when needed.

Another challenge is how to handle the guilt or shame of avoiding negative people. It's important to remember that you have the right to take care of yourself and surround yourself with positivity. Avoiding negative people is not a sign of weakness, but rather a sign of strength and self-care.

Negative people can have a significant impact on our overall well-being. However, by understanding and avoiding negative people, we can improve our mental and physical health. Incorporating strategies such as setting boundaries, practising mindfulness, and seeking support can help avoid negative people and maintain a positive mindset.

Remember to also practise self-compassion and be kind to yourself during the process of overcoming negative people. And always remember that you have the power to choose the people you surround yourself with and it is your responsibility to take care of yourself.

15

Breaking Free: Strategies For Overcoming Negative Thoughts

Negative thoughts can have a significant impact on our mental and physical health. They can lead to feelings of hopelessness and helplessness, increased risk of mental health issues such as anxiety and depression, and even physical health problems. To improve our overall well-being, it's important to address and overcome negative thoughts.

In this chapter, we will discuss strategies for identifying and overcoming negative thoughts. We'll also explore the underlying causes of negative thinking, including the role of past experiences and trauma, and offer tips for maintaining a positive mindset in the long term.

Strategies for overcoming negative thoughts

Several techniques can be used to identify and challenge negative thoughts. One of the most effective techniques is cognitive restructuring, which involves identifying and challenging negative thoughts and replacing them with more positive and realistic thoughts.

Positive affirmations and self-talk can also help replace negative thoughts. Mindfulness practices such as meditation and focusing on the present moment can also help one become more aware of negative thoughts and learn to let them go. In addition, self-compassion and being kind to oneself during the process of overcoming negative thoughts can be beneficial.

Tips for maintaining a positive mindset

Building a support system and seeking help when needed, such as therapy or counselling, can help maintain a positive mindset. Finding inspiration and motivation through role models and success stories can also be beneficial. Practising resilience and learning from past experiences can also be helpful. Incorporating stress-management techniques such as exercise, relaxation, and meditation can also be beneficial in maintaining a positive mindset.

Addressing triggers: Negative thoughts can often be triggered by certain situations or events. It's important to identify these triggers and have strategies in place to handle them. This may include developing a plan of action, practising mindfulness, or seeking support from a therapist or counsellor.

Negative thoughts can have a significant impact on our overall well-being. However, by identifying and addressing negative thoughts, we can learn to overcome them and improve our mental and physical health. Incorporating strategies such as cognitive restructuring, positive affirmations, mindfulness, and self-compassion can help overcome negative thoughts.

Remember to also seek support when needed and to address triggers that lead to negative thoughts. The journey to a positive mindset takes time and effort but with the right approach, it is achievable.

Understanding the role that past experiences and trauma play in the development of negative thoughts and seeking appropriate support can be crucial in overcoming negative thinking patterns.

Step outside your comfort zone ... even just a little bit and feel amazing!

16

Stepping Out Of Your Comfort Zone

The comfort zone is a psychological concept that refers to the familiar and safe areas of our lives where we feel secure and in control. It's the place where we feel comfortable and confident in our abilities, and where we tend to spend most of our time.

However, while the comfort zone can provide a sense of security, it can also limit our growth and potential. Coming out of our comfort zones can be scary and uncomfortable, but it also has the potential to bring about significant benefits.

Examples of activities and situations that may be considered part of someone's comfort zone could include:

- A specific job or career.
- A familiar social setting.
- A set of hobbies or activities.
- A certain way of thinking and behaving.

The benefits of coming out of your comfort zone

While the comfort zone can provide a sense of security, it can also limit our growth and potential. By stepping out of our comfort zones, we expose ourselves to new and different experiences, which can bring about significant benefits.

These include:

Personal growth: Coming out of our comfort zones allows us to challenge ourselves, learn new things, and gain new perspectives. This can lead to personal growth and self-improvement.

Increased confidence: By facing and overcoming challenges, we can build self-confidence and self-esteem.

Improved problem-solving skills: When we're faced with new and unfamiliar situations, we have to think on our feet and come up with creative solutions. This can help to improve our problem-solving skills and make us more adaptable in the face of change.

Increased creativity: Stepping out of our comfort zones can help to stimulate our brains and inspire new ideas and ways of thinking.

How people feel before and after coming out of their comfort zone

It's normal to feel some level of anxiety or discomfort when faced with new and unfamiliar situations. However, with time and practice, most people find that they can push through these initial feelings and come out on the other side with a sense of accomplishment and self-confidence.

Some people may feel:

- Nervous or anxious before taking the step out of their comfort zone.
- Excitement and anticipation for the new experience.
- A sense of accomplishment and pride after successfully stepping out of their comfort zone.
- Increased confidence in their abilities and willingness to take on new challenges in the future.

Many different situations and scenarios can prompt someone to come out of their comfort zone. Some examples include:

- Starting a new job or career.
- Moving to a new city or country.
- Taking on a new hobby or activity.
- Joining a new group or club.
- Starting a new relationship.
- Making a major life change.

How you can start today

Coming out of your comfort zone can be a daunting task, but it's important to remember that it doesn't have to be a huge, life-altering change. Here are a few simple steps you can take to start small:

- Start with small, manageable steps.
- Identify the things that make you feel uncomfortable and challenge yourself to face them.
- Take baby steps and make small changes that will lead to bigger changes in the future.
- Surround yourself with a supportive network of friends and family who will encourage and motivate you.
- Practise mindfulness and focus on the present moment.

This can help to reduce feelings of anxiety and stress when stepping out of your comfort zone.

Remember that failure is a natural part of the process. Don't be discouraged by setbacks and view them as opportunities for growth.

It's important to remember that coming out of your comfort zone is a process and it's okay to take it one step at a time.

Start small and gradually increase the level of challenge as you become more comfortable. Keep in mind that the benefits of coming out of your comfort zone can be immense, so don't be afraid to take the first step today.

25 small ways anybody can come out of their comfort zone today

1. Try a new food or cuisine.
2. Take a different route to work or school.
3. Start a conversation with a stranger.
4. Take a class or workshop on something you've always been curious about.
5. Take a different form of transportation than you usually do.
6. Attend a networking event or meet-up.
7. Sign up for a volunteer opportunity.
8. Speak up in a meeting or presentation.
9. Take a solo trip or vacation.
10. Start a new hobby or activity.
11. Listen to a different type of music than you usually do.
12. Go to a live event or performance alone.
13. Take a different fitness class than you usually do.
14. Start a conversation with someone you've never talked to before.
15. Try a new type of workout or exercise.
16. Read a book or watch a movie outside of your usual genre.
17. Take a different approach to a work or school project.
18. Go to a different grocery store or shopping centre.

19. Take on a new responsibility at work or in your personal life.
20. Join a new club or group.
21. Take a day trip to a nearby city or town.
22. Try a new type of cuisine or restaurant.
23. Take a different approach to a problem or challenge you're facing.
24. Take a different approach in a personal or professional relationship.
25. Step out of your usual routine and try something new and different.

How will this help me feel more positive?

Stepping out of your comfort zone and trying new things can have a positive impact on your overall well-being in several ways:

Sense of accomplishment: By facing and overcoming challenges, you can build self-confidence and self-esteem, and have a sense of accomplishment.

Improved problem-solving skills: When you're faced with new and unfamiliar situations, you have to think on your feet and come up with creative solutions. This can help to improve your problem-solving skills and make you more adaptable in the face of change, which can help you to feel more positive.

Increased creativity: Stepping out of your comfort zone can help to stimulate your brain and inspire new ideas and ways of thinking. This can help you to feel more positive and inspired.

Personal growth: Coming out of your comfort zone allows you to challenge yourself, learn new things, and gain new perspectives. This can lead to personal growth and self-improvement, which can help you to feel more positive.

Increased social connections: By stepping out of your comfort zone, you expose yourself to new people, which can lead to increased social connections and a sense of community, which can also make you feel more positive.

New experiences: Trying new things can help you to have new experiences, which can help to broaden your perspective and make you feel more positive.

Increased self-awareness: By trying new things and stepping out of your comfort zone, you may gain a better understanding of yourself and your abilities, which can lead to increased self-awareness and a sense of self-acceptance which can help to make you feel more positive.

Breaking monotony: Breaking the monotony of doing the same things over and over again can help you to feel more positive and excited about life.

Overall, stepping out of your comfort zone can help you to feel more positive by providing opportunities for growth, learning, and new experiences, and by increasing self-awareness, self-confidence and creativity.

17

Limiting Beliefs

Limiting beliefs are those that hold us back in life, preventing us from reaching our goals and fulfilling our potential. They can manifest in many different forms, such as "I'm not good enough," "I'll never be successful," "I can't change," and "I'm not worthy." These beliefs can be deeply ingrained in our minds and can be difficult to overcome, but it is essential to understand them and learn how to challenge them to live a fulfilling and successful life.

Limiting beliefs is often rooted in past experiences or negative messages that we have internalised from others. These beliefs can be self-imposed or imposed by others and can be related to any aspect of life, such as relationships, career, or personal growth.

Do you have limiting beliefs?

Several signs may indicate that you have limiting beliefs:

Negative self-talk: If you find yourself frequently engaging in negative self-talk, such as saying things like "I'm not good enough,"

"I'll never be successful," or "I can't change," it may be a sign that you have limiting beliefs.

Avoiding certain situations or activities: If you find yourself avoiding certain situations or activities because you believe you can't do them or won't be successful, it may be a sign that you have limiting beliefs.

Lack of confidence or self-esteem: If you struggle with low confidence or self-esteem, it may be a sign that you have limiting beliefs about yourself and your abilities.

Difficulty setting or achieving goals: If you find it difficult to set or achieve goals, it may be a sign that you have limiting beliefs about your abilities and potential.

Difficulty forming healthy relationships: If you find it difficult to form healthy relationships, it may be a sign that you have limiting beliefs about yourself and your worthiness of love and connection.

Difficulty in career development: If you find it difficult to advance in your career or have a hard time finding a job, it may be a sign that you have limiting beliefs about your abilities and potential.

It's important to note that everyone has some limiting beliefs and they are not necessarily bad, but when they become a hindrance to our daily lives, it's important to recognise them and work on changing them.

Some examples of common limiting beliefs include:

- "I'm not smart enough"
- "I'll never be able to afford that"
- "I'm not attractive enough"
- "I'm not good enough"

- "I'll never be successful"
- "I can't change"
- "I'm not worthy"

It is important to understand that limiting beliefs are not necessarily true and that they are often based on false assumptions or past experiences that no longer apply to our current situation.

Where do limiting beliefs come from?

Limiting beliefs can come from a variety of sources, including past experiences, negative messages we've internalised from others, or societal expectations and stereotypes.

Past experiences: Limiting beliefs can be formed from past experiences, such as traumatic events, failed attempts, or past rejections. These experiences can create negative associations and beliefs that can persist in our minds and hold us back in the future.

Negative messages from others: We may have internalised negative messages from others, such as parents, teachers, peers, or media. These messages can shape our beliefs about ourselves and our abilities and can be difficult to change without recognising their origin.

Societal expectations and stereotypes: Limiting beliefs can also come from societal expectations and stereotypes. For example, if we believe that men should not cry or that women are not good at math, it can hold us back from achieving our goals and reaching our full potential.

Repetitive patterns: Often limiting beliefs are formed from patterns that repeat in our life. If we have a repetitive pattern of failure, rejection or disappointment, it can shape our beliefs about our ability to succeed and can make it hard for us to change the pattern.

It's important to recognise that limiting beliefs can come from a variety of sources and can be deeply ingrained in our minds.

By understanding where our limiting beliefs come from, we can better understand how to challenge and overcome them. It can be helpful to reflect on our past experiences, to think about the influences of the people around us and the societal messages we've received, and to look for patterns in our life that might have shaped our beliefs.

The impact of limiting beliefs

Limiting beliefs can have a significant impact on our confidence, self-esteem, and overall well-being. They can manifest in different areas of our lives, including relationships, careers, and personal growth.

The role of limiting beliefs is creating a self-fulfilling prophecy, where our beliefs shape our actions and ultimately lead us to the very outcome we feared. For example, if we believe we are not good enough, we may not even try to apply for the job we want, and in turn, we will not get it.

Research has shown that limiting beliefs can lead to increased stress, anxiety, and depression. They can also affect our ability to form healthy relationships and can hinder our career progress. To overcome limiting beliefs, it is essential to understand the impact they have on our lives and take steps to challenge them.

Strategies for overcoming limiting beliefs

Several strategies can be used to overcome limiting beliefs. These include:

Identifying and challenging limiting beliefs through self-

reflection and mindfulness. Take some time to reflect on the beliefs that hold you back, and challenge them by asking yourself whether they are true.

Taking action towards your goal, even if it's small, can help to challenge and change your limiting beliefs.

It is important to note that overcoming limiting beliefs can be a challenging process, and it may take time and effort.

However, the benefits of doing so are well worth the effort, as they can lead to increased confidence, self-esteem, and overall well-being. They can also open up new opportunities and possibilities in our lives, and empower us to take control of our lives and reach our full potential.

If you're looking to challenge your limiting beliefs today, there are several steps you can take:

Identify your limiting beliefs: Take some time to reflect on the beliefs that hold you back. These can be related to any aspect of your life, such as relationships, career, or personal growth. Write them down and be specific.

Challenge the evidence: Once you have identified your limiting beliefs, ask yourself whether they are true. Challenge the evidence by looking for counter-examples, researching or looking for facts that contradict your belief.

Reframe your thoughts: Once you have identified and challenged your limiting beliefs, try reframing them in a more positive light. For example, instead of saying *"I'm not good enough,"* try saying *"I am worthy, capable and strong."*

The value of overcoming limiting beliefs

The value of overcoming limiting beliefs cannot be overstated. When we overcome limiting beliefs, we open ourselves up to new opportunities and possibilities in life. We become more confident, self-assured, and capable of achieving our goals. We also become more resilient, better able to handle life's challenges, and more able to form healthy relationships.

Research has also shown that overcoming limiting beliefs can lead to improved mental health, well-being, and success. A study by the University of California found that individuals who were able to overcome limiting beliefs experienced a decrease in stress and an increase in self-esteem and life satisfaction. Additionally, a study by the University of London found that individuals who were able to overcome limiting beliefs were more likely to achieve their goals and experience greater success in their careers.

Limiting beliefs can hold us back in life, preventing us from reaching our full potential. However, by understanding and challenging these beliefs, we can overcome them and open ourselves up to new opportunities and possibilities. We can become more confident, self-assured, and capable of achieving our goals. Additionally, it is important to surround ourselves with positive and supportive people and take action towards our goals. Remember that change is possible, and it starts with recognising and addressing our limiting beliefs.

18

What If Our Parents Influenced Our Limiting Beliefs?

One of the sources of these limiting beliefs can be our parents. Our parents play a crucial role in shaping our beliefs and attitudes and can have a significant impact on our self-esteem, self-worth, and overall well-being. Unfortunately, sometimes, parents can negatively influence us and may have passed down limiting beliefs that have held us back in life.

Understanding the root causes

Limiting beliefs can be formed in childhood through messages and behaviours learned from parents. These messages and behaviours can shape our beliefs about ourselves and our abilities and can be difficult to change without recognising their origin.

One of the root causes of these limiting beliefs is negative parenting styles. Negative parenting styles can include criticism, lack of validation, or unrealistic expectations. These parenting styles can make us feel inadequate and unworthy and can lead to the development of limiting beliefs.

Additionally, past experiences and traumas within the family can shape our beliefs. For example, if a child grows up in an environment where they were repeatedly told they were not good enough, they may internalise this belief and carry it into adulthood.

Signs and symptoms of parent-influenced limiting beliefs

Examples of limiting beliefs that may be influenced by parents include "I'm not good enough," "I'll never be successful," "I'm not worthy," etc. These beliefs can have a significant impact on our lives and may have shown themselves in our childhood in various ways.

For example, if we had difficulty forming relationships, had low self-esteem, or had difficulty setting and achieving goals, it could be a sign that we have parent-influenced limiting beliefs. These beliefs can continue to affect us in our adult lives and relationships.

The consequences of not challenging parent-influenced limiting beliefs

If we don't challenge these parent-influenced limiting beliefs, they can hold us back in life and prevent us from reaching our full potential. These beliefs can create a self-fulfilling prophecy, where our beliefs shape our actions and ultimately lead us to the very outcome we feared.

Additionally, they can have a significant impact on our mental health and well-being, leading to increased stress, anxiety, and depression.

Strategies for overcoming parent-influenced limiting beliefs

To overcome parent-influenced limiting beliefs, it is important to first identify and challenge these beliefs through self-reflection and mindfulness. This means taking the time to reflect on the beliefs that hold you back and asking yourself whether they are true.

Cognitive-behavioural techniques, such as positive affirmations and visualisation, can also be effective in challenging limiting beliefs. Instead of saying, "I'm not good enough," try saying "I am worthy, capable and strong." This can help to re-wire our brains and shift our mindset.

Another strategy for overcoming limiting beliefs is seeking therapy or coaching. A therapist or coach can help you work through your limiting beliefs, your past, and your relationship with your parents and provide you with strategies.

Surrounding yourself with supportive and positive people can also help to challenge limiting beliefs. The people we surround ourselves with can have a significant impact on our beliefs and attitudes. Surrounding ourselves with positive, supportive people can help us to develop a more positive outlook on life.

Repairing the relationship

To repair the relationship with our parents and overcome limiting beliefs, it's important to understand the root causes of these beliefs. This means being able to forgive and empathise with our parents, and understanding that they may have passed down limiting beliefs without realising it.

Open and honest communication with our parents can also be beneficial in repairing the relationship and understanding where these limiting beliefs came from. Additionally, setting healthy boundaries and learning to separate ourselves from our parent's beliefs and attitudes can also help in this process.

Parent-influenced limiting beliefs can hold us back in life and prevent us from reaching our full potential. However, by understanding and challenging these beliefs, we can overcome them and open ourselves up to new opportunities and possibilities.

It's important to take the time to reflect on these beliefs, challenge the evidence, and seek professional help if needed. Repairing the relationship with our parents and setting healthy boundaries can also be beneficial in overcoming limiting beliefs.

19

Pursue Your Passions - Be A Kid Again!

Adopting a "be a kid again" mindset can help you feel more positive in your everyday adult life in several ways:

Increased happiness and joy: Engaging in activities that you loved as a child can bring back feelings of nostalgia and happiness. This can help improve your overall mood and can make you feel more positive and energised.

Reduced stress: Engaging in activities that you loved as a child can be a form of escapism. It can provide a mental break from the stressors of adult life and can help you feel more relaxed and at ease.

Improved mood: Engaging in activities that you loved as a child can release endorphins, which are the body's natural mood boosters. This can help improve your overall mood and can make you feel more positive and energised.

Increased creativity: Engaging in activities that you loved as a child can help tap into your inner child and can help you reconnect with your imagination and creativity. This can be especially beneficial for those who feel stuck in a rut or are struggling with creative blocks.

Improved relationships: Engaging in activities that you loved as a child can be a fun and bonding experience to share with others. It can provide a way to connect with friends, family, or loved ones, and can help strengthen relationships.

Increased self-awareness: Engaging in activities that you loved as a child can help you identify what you enjoy and what makes you happy. It can provide you with a sense of self-awareness and can help you understand what you want and need in life.

Improved physical health: Activities that you loved as a child can also be a form of exercise, such as playing sports or climbing, which can help improve your physical health.

By incorporating these activities that you loved as a child into your everyday life, you can help create a more positive and balanced lifestyle. It's important to note that it's not necessary to engage in these activities all the time but taking time out of your day to engage in activities that you loved as a child can help you feel more positive and energised.

20

Why Do We Feel We Can't "Be A Kid?"

There are a few reasons why some adults may feel guilty about "being a kid again":

Societal pressure: Society often places a lot of pressure on adults to act and behave a certain way. There is a perception that adults should be serious and focused on responsibilities, rather than engaging in activities that are seen as "childish" or "frivolous."

Fear of judgment: Some adults may be afraid of what others will think if they engage in activities that are associated with being a child. They may worry about being judged for not being mature enough or for being seen as irresponsible.

Lack of time: Some adults may feel that they simply don't have the time to engage in activities that they loved as a child. They may feel that their responsibilities take precedence and that there is no time for "childish" activities.

Self-doubt: Some adults may feel that they're not good at the activities they loved as a child, or that they've lost the skills they once had. They may feel that they're not capable of enjoying these activities as adults, which can prevent them from even trying.

Money issues: Some adults may feel guilty about spending money on activities that they loved as a child, as they feel it's not a good use of their money. They may feel they should be saving the money for more important things.

However, it's important to remember that engaging in activities that you loved as a child is not only normal but also beneficial for your well-being. Society's expectations and pressure from others should not dictate how you spend your free time.

You deserve to enjoy your life and find balance in it. It's also important to note that you can still engage in these activities while also taking care of responsibilities and managing your finances.

21

Hobby Ideas To Live A More Positive Life

Here is a list of ideas you could start today to incorporate a positive activity in your life.

Pick 2-3 and start having fun! You never know where it may take you!

Gardening: Gardening can be a relaxing and rewarding hobby. It can help you connect with nature, improve your physical health, and boost your mood.

Painting: Painting can be a great way to express yourself creatively and can help reduce stress.

Photography: Photography can be a great way to capture the beauty of the world around you and can help you appreciate the small things in life.

Yoga: Yoga can help improve your physical and mental well-being, reduce stress, and increase your sense of inner peace.

Reading: Reading can help improve your concentration, boost your memory, and take you on a journey without leaving your home.

Cooking: Cooking can be a fun and rewarding hobby. It can help you explore new flavours, improve your health and nutrition, and give you a sense of accomplishment.

Dancing: Dancing can be a great way to let loose, improve your physical health, and boost your mood.

Hiking: Hiking can be a great way to get outside, improve your physical health, and connect with nature.

Writing: Writing can be a great way to express yourself creatively and can help you process your thoughts and emotions.

Knitting: Knitting can be a relaxing and meditative hobby that can help improve your focus and concentration.

Running: Running can be a great way to improve your physical health, reduce stress, and boost your mood.

Fishing: Fishing can be a peaceful and relaxing hobby that can help you connect with nature and improve your focus and concentration.

Swimming: Swimming can be a great way to improve your physical health and boost your mood.

Scrapbooking: Scrapbooking can be a fun and creative way to preserve memories and express yourself.

Singing: Singing can be a great way to let loose, improve your mood, and boost your confidence.

Rock climbing: Rock climbing can be a great way to improve your physical health, boost your confidence, and push your limits.

Biking: Biking can be a great way to improve your physical health, reduce stress, and explore your local area.

Skateboarding: Skateboarding can be a great way to improve your physical health, boost your confidence, and have fun.

Surfing: Surfing can be a great way to improve your physical health, boost your mood, and connect with nature.

Board games: Board games can be a great way to spend time with friends and family, improve your problem-solving skills, and have fun.

Journaling: Journaling can be a great way to process your thoughts and emotions, reflect on your experiences, and set goals for the future.

Origami: Origami can be a relaxing and meditative hobby that can help improve your focus and concentration.

Pottery: Pottery can be a great way to express yourself creatively and improve your fine motor skills.

Calligraphy: Calligraphy can be a great way to improve your handwriting, express yourself creatively, and create beautiful works of art.

Woodworking: Woodworking can be a great way to improve your problem-solving skills, boost your confidence, and create beautiful and functional objects.

Sewing: Sewing can be a great way to express yourself creatively, improve your fine motor skills, and create your own clothes and accessories.

Quilting: Quilting can be a relaxing and meditative hobby that can help improve your focus and concentration.

Glassblowing: Glassblowing can be a great way to express yourself creatively and create beautiful and unique works of art.

Model building: Model building can be a great way to improve your problem-solving skills, boost your confidence, and create beautiful and detailed models.

Building with LEGOS: Building with LEGOS can be a great way to improve your problem-solving skills, boost your creativity, and have fun.

Geocaching: Geocaching can be a great way to explore your local area, improve your problem-solving skills, and have fun with friends and family.

Stargazing: Stargazing can be a great way to improve your concentration, learn more about astronomy, and appreciate the beauty of the night sky.

Playing an Instrument: Playing an instrument can be a great way to express yourself creatively, improve your fine motor skills, and boost your mood.

Learning a new language: Learning a new language can improve your cognitive abilities, open up new opportunities, and help you communicate with people from different cultures.

Travelling: Traveling can be a great way to explore new places, learn about different cultures, and broaden your perspective on the world.

Volunteer work: Volunteer work can be a great way to give back to your community, meet new people, and make a positive impact on the world.

Meditation: Meditation can help reduce stress, improve your focus and concentration, and boost your mood.

Tai Chi: Tai Chi can be a great way to improve your physical health, reduce stress, and boost your mood.

Playing sports: Playing sports can be a great way to improve your physical health, boost your confidence, and have fun with friends and family.

Playing video games: Playing video games can be a great way to have fun, improve your problem-solving skills, and spend time with friends and family.

Building a model aeroplane: Building a model aeroplane can be a great way to improve your problem-solving skills, boost your confidence, and create a beautiful and functional model.

Building a model train: Building a model train can be a great way to improve your problem-solving skills, boost your confidence, and create a beautiful and functional model.

Building a model boat: Building a model boat can be a great way to improve your problem-solving skills, boost your confidence, and create a beautiful and functional model.

22

Create A Bucket List - Feel Amazing!

Creating a bucket list can make you feel amazing for several reasons.

First, it gives you a sense of purpose and direction. Having a list of goals and experiences that you want to accomplish can provide a clear roadmap for your life, and give you something to work towards. This can increase your motivation, and help you stay focused on what's truly important to you.

Second, it can help you prioritise your time and energy. By creating a bucket list, you can identify the activities and experiences that are most important to you, and make sure that you're spending your time and energy on the things that truly matter.

Third, it can help you live in the present moment. By focusing on the things you want to accomplish in the future, you can start to appreciate the present moment more fully. This can help you enjoy the journey, rather than just focusing on the destination.

Lastly, it can make you feel amazing because it allows you to dream big, to dream of things you never thought possible, and to have something to look forward to. It gives you a sense of hope and excitement and can create a positive sense of accomplishment as you start to cross things off your list.

Creating a bucket list can be a powerful tool for personal growth, self-discovery, and achieving your goals. It can help you stay focused on what's truly important, and help you live a more fulfilling and meaningful life.

Some myths about creating a bucket list

Myth 1: A bucket list is only for older people nearing the end of their lives.

Truth: A bucket list is for people of all ages and stages of life. It's never too early or late to start thinking about the experiences and goals you want to accomplish in your lifetime.

Myth 2: A bucket list has to be expensive or require a lot of resources.

Truth: A bucket list can include a mix of big and small experiences and goals, and they don't have to be expensive. Many bucket list items can be accomplished on a budget, or even for free.

Myth 3: A bucket list has to be set in stone and can't be changed.

Truth: A bucket list is a living document, and it can be changed, edited or updated as your priorities, interests, or life circumstances change.

Myth 4: A bucket list is only for the adventurous.

Truth: A bucket list is for everyone, regardless of their level of adventure. It can include both adventurous and sedate experiences, depending on your preferences.

Myth 5: A bucket list is only about material possessions and experiences.

Truth: A bucket list can include both material and non-material items such as personal development, self-care, and spiritual growth.

Some bucket list ideas

Pick 3-5 and start working towards them today!

- Travel to a foreign country.
- Learn a new language.
- Climb a mountain.
- Go on a safari.
- Swim with sharks.
- Go bungee jumping.
- Take a hot air balloon ride.
- Go skydiving.
- Visit all 50 states in the US.
- Go on a cruise.
- Attend a music festival.
- Go to a concert of your favourite band.
- Visit the Seven Wonders of the World.
- Go on a road trip across the country.
- Take a cooking class.
- Go to a wine tasting.
- Attend a film festival.
- Visit Disneyland or Disney World.
- Attend a sporting event at a famous stadium.
- Go to a Broadway show.
- Visit the Grand Canyon.
- Go scuba diving.
- Take a hot air balloon ride.
- Go to a spa for a weekend.
- Visit a castle.
- Go to a zoo.

- Attend a comedy show.
- Take a dance class.
- Go to a museum.
- Go to a theme park.
- Take a pottery class.
- Go to a botanical garden.
- Take a photography class.
- Go to a water park.
- Attend a professional development conference.
- Go on a hike.
- Take a painting class.
- Visit a national park.
- Attend a book club.
- Go to a farmer's market.
- Take a gardening class.
- Go to a beach.
- Take a yoga class.
- Visit a historical site.
- Go to an aquarium.
- Take a writing class.
- Go to an amusement park.
- Attend a networking event.
- Volunteer at a charity.
- Start a daily gratitude journal.
- Attend a live stand-up comedy show.
- Go to a concert of your favourite band.
- Go on a hike.

23

Writing A Priority List

A priority list is a list of tasks, goals or objectives that are ranked in order of importance. It helps individuals or organisations to focus on the most important tasks and make sure they are completed before moving on to less important ones. It helps to prioritise and manage time and resources effectively and can be used to set short-term or long-term goals. It can also be used to track progress and measure success. Priority lists can be created in many forms, such as written lists, spreadsheets, or project management software, and can be used in personal or professional settings.

Why is a priority list more effective than a long to-do list?

Priority lists are more effective than to-do lists because they help to focus on the most important tasks first. When we have a long to-do list, it can be easy to get overwhelmed and not know where to start. This can lead to procrastination and a lack of motivation. However, when we prioritise our tasks, we know exactly what needs to be done first, and we can tackle it with a sense of purpose and direction.

Priority lists also help us to manage our time more effectively. By focusing on the most important tasks first, we can ensure that we are using our time in the most productive way possible. Additionally, when we prioritise tasks, we can better allocate our resources such as time and energy to the most important items.

Moreover, priority lists allow us to track our progress and measure our success. We can see what we have accomplished and what still needs to be done. This can help to increase motivation and give us a sense of accomplishment.

In addition, by prioritising our tasks, we can help to minimise stress and increase productivity. When we know what needs to be done, we can focus on completing those tasks and avoid getting bogged down in less important tasks.

Overall, priority lists are more effective than to-do lists because they help us to focus on the most important tasks, manage our time more effectively, track progress, measure success, minimise stress and increase productivity.

Your weekly/monthly priority list

Health:

- Exercise for at least 30 minutes every day.
- Meal prep for the week on Sunday.
- Take a daily walk outside.
- Make a doctor's appointment for a check-up.
- Try a new healthy recipe every week.

Business:

- Follow up on leads and schedule meetings with potential clients.
- Complete weekly financial report.
- Work on a business plan for a new project.

- Attend a workshop or conference related to your field.
- Schedule a meeting with a mentor or coach.

Socialising:

- Schedule a weekly phone call with a friend or family member.
- Attend a networking event once a month.
- Organise a monthly get-together with friends.
- Plan a vacation with friends or family.
- Volunteer for a community event.

Creative Activities:

- Spend 30 minutes working on a personal project every day.
- Spend an hour on a creative hobby every Saturday.
- Take a painting class once a month.
- Sign up for a writing workshop.
- Start a daily journaling practice.

As you can see, now the priority list is more organised and easy to follow. You can focus on one aspect at a time, and track your progress. This way, you'll have a better idea of what you are doing, and what still needs to be done.

You will feel amazing by incorporating these into your priority list. Of course, housework needs to be done, but you will see what happens when we filter this further into a new daily routine that will be your priority list.

Your new daily/weekly priority list could look like this:

Monday:

- Health - Exercise for at least 30 minutes.

- Business - Follow up on leads and schedule meetings with potential clients.
- Socialising - Schedule a weekly phone call with a friend or family member.
- Creative activities - Spend 30 minutes working on a personal project.

Tuesday:

- Health - Meal prep for the week.
- Business - Complete weekly financial report.
- Socialising - Attend a networking event.
- Creative activities - Spend an hour on a creative hobby.

Wednesday:

- Health - Take a daily walk outside.
- Business - Work on a business plan for a new project.
- Socialising - Organise a monthly get-together with friends.
- Creative activities - Take a painting class.

Thursday:

- Health - Make a doctor's appointment for a check-up.
- Business - Attend a workshop or conference related to your field.
- Socialising - Plan a vacation with friends or family.
- Creative activities - Sign up for a writing workshop.

Friday:

- Health - Try a new healthy recipe every week.
- Business - Schedule a meeting with a mentor or coach.
- Socialising - Volunteer for a community event.
- Creative activities - Start a daily journaling practice.

Saturday:

- Health - Take a yoga class.
- Business - Review and update business plan.
- Socialising - Organise a dinner with friends.
- Creative activities - Spend 2 hours on a creative hobby.

Sunday:

- Health - Cook a healthy meal.
- Business - Prepare for the upcoming week.
- Socialising - Spend time with family.
- Creative activities - Write in journal for 30 min.

Can you see, you only have 4 things on your list and each one enriches you in some way.

I can hear you say *'but I have kids and need to do the housework'*.

And it can seem daunting, can't it, but doing little and often (yes, even setting a timer for doing your housework, put some earphones on and enjoy listening to your favourite music!)

If you have children, take a look at this:

Monday:

- Health - Exercise for at least 30 minutes.
- Business - Follow up on leads and schedule meetings with potential clients.
- Socialising - Schedule a weekly phone call with a friend or family member.
- Creative activities - Spend 30 minutes working on a personal project.
- Family - Take kids to and from school.
- Cleaning - Clean for 15 minutes (use a timer, put some music on).

Tuesday:

- Health - Meal prep for the week.
- Business - Complete weekly financial report.
- Socialising - Attend a networking event.
- Creative activities - Spend an hour on a creative hobby.
- Family - Take kids to and from school.
- Cleaning - Clean for 15 minutes (use a timer, put some music on).

Wednesday:

- Health - Take a daily walk outside.
- Business - Work on a business plan for a new project.
- Socialising - Organise a monthly get-together with friends.
- Creative activities - Take a painting class.
- Family - Take kids to and from school.
- Cleaning - Clean for 15 minutes (use a timer, put some music on).

Thursday:

- Health - Make a doctor's appointment for a check-up.
- Business - Attend a workshop or conference related to your field.
- Socialising - Plan a vacation/day out with friends or family.
- Creative activities - Sign up for a writing workshop.
- Family - Take kids to and from school.
- Cleaning - Clean for 15 minutes (use a timer, put some music on).

Friday:

- Health - Try a new healthy recipe every week.
- Business - Schedule a meeting with a mentor or coach.

- Socialising - Volunteer for a community event.
- Creative activities - Start a daily journaling practice.
- Family - Take kids to and from school.
- Cleaning - Clean for 15 minutes (use a timer, put some music on).

Saturday:

- Health - Take a yoga class.
- Business - Review and update business plan.
- Socialising - Organise a dinner with friends.
- Creative activities - Spend 2 hours on a creative hobby.
- Family - Spend quality time with the family.
- Cleaning - Clean for 15 minutes (use a timer, put some music on).

Sunday:

- Health - Cook a healthy meal.
- Business - Prepare for the upcoming week.
- Socialising - Spend time with family.
- Creative activities - Write in journal for 30 min.
- Family - Spend quality time with the family.
- Cleaning - Clean for 15 minutes (use a timer, put some music on).

Yes, it really can be that simple.

We are conditioned that it is only acceptable if we are 'busy' and 'tired' all the time and somehow feel guilty for prioritising ourselves and our own enjoyment.

That stops now.

You bought this book because you wanted to feel more positive, right?

It starts with simplicity and cutting a lot of stuff out. And it will feel strange. But investing in yourself will be the best thing for you and your family.

Try it.

Make a priority list – NOT a to-do list.

Incorporate something from the 'health, fitness, family, creative, business' list and see which day you prefer to do certain activities.

But by having 4-5 things on our 'priority list' seems a lot more doable than 25 things right?

The night before, literally say:

'If I did nothing else tomorrow, what would move me forward in health, wealth, family, fitness and creativity'

And do that – it's that simple.

24

Conclusion

Thinking more positively is a journey that requires effort and commitment. However, by understanding the root causes of limiting beliefs, challenging them with CBT techniques, and setting priorities that align with our goals and values, we can make significant progress towards a more fulfilling and happier life.

One of the key takeaways from this book is the importance of stepping out of our comfort zones and embracing new experiences. Whether it's trying a new hobby, travelling to a new place, or meeting new people, these experiences can help us to grow, learn and develop a more positive outlook.

Another important aspect of positive thinking is to embrace the inner child within us. By enjoying the things we loved when we were younger, we can tap into a sense of wonder and joy that can bring more positivity and happiness to our daily lives.

As we have seen throughout this book, there are many practical strategies and techniques that we can use to improve our mental well-being. By incorporating these strategies into our daily lives, and being mindful of the way we think and feel, we can achieve a more positive and fulfilling life.

By understanding and addressing our limiting beliefs, setting priorities, and embracing new experiences, we can break free from our comfort zones, and achieve our goals, with a positive and happy mindset. We hope this book has helped you to understand the power of positive thinking and how you can use it to design the life you deserve.

Take care and all the best for a creative, adventurous, happy and fulfilling life!

Other books By Rachel Stone

Develop the power of positive thinking TODAY!

Other books by Rachel Stone

RACHEL STONE
WHAT CONFIDENT Women Do

9 STEPS TO ULTIMATE SELF-CONFIDENCE

Discover the 9 steps to ultimate self-confidence
TODAY!

Other books by Rachel Stone

Stop people-pleasing and doubting. A friendly guide to dealing with toxic relationships and gaslighting. Start living, healing and being the best version of yourself TODAY!

Other books by Rachel Stone

Get the tools to break free from self-absorbed and emotionally abusive family members. Let go of the need for approval and learn to love yourself. Embark on a journey of acceptance and be happy again TODAY!

Other books by Rachel Stone

Get anxiety relief from people-pleasing. Stop dimming your light for others. Dare to set boundaries and live your best life with courage, freedom and without apologies TODAY!

Other books by Rachel Stone

RACHEL STONE
WHY LIVING A SIMPLE LIFE IS BETTER *For You*

THROUGH DECLUTTERING, MINIMALISM AND STREAMLINING, FINALLY START ENJOYING A MEANINGFUL LIFE

Through decluttering, minimalism and streamlining, finally start enjoying a meaningful life TODAY!

Other books by Rachel Stone

Get your friendly guide to living a fabulous life feeling free and happy TODAY!

Other books by Rachel Stone

Stop your negative thinking in its tracks. New practical strategies to master your mind and block your intrusive thoughts, even if you've tried it all before. Take back control TODAY!

www.ingramcontent.com/pod-product-compliance
Lightning Source LLC
Chambersburg PA
CBHW050247120526
44590CB00016B/2250